HOW TO BUILD A HUMAN BODY

TOM JACKSON

SCHOLASTIC

Scholastic Children's Books
Euston House, 24 Eversholt Street,
London, NW1 1DB, UK

A division of Scholastic Ltd
London – New York – Toronto – Sydney – Auckland
– Mexico City – New Delhi – Hong Kong

Editorial Project Manager: Jill Sawyer
Assistant Editor: Corinne Lucas

Developed for Scholastic by
Brown Bear Books Ltd.:
Designer: Siobhan Gallagher
Additional Illustrations: Arvind Shah
Senior Managing Editor: Tim Cooke
Children's Publisher: Anne O'Daly

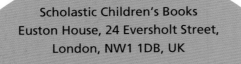
First published in the UK by Scholastic Ltd, 2013
Book concept copyright © Brown Bear Books Ltd
© Scholastic Ltd, 2013
Cover illustrations © Clive Goddard, 2013
All rights reserved

ISBN 978 1407 13737 7

Printed and bound in Singapore by Tien Wah Press

2 4 6 8 10 9 7 5 3 1

CONTENTS

THIS BOOK

Ever been inside a body? Well, that's where we're heading. Prepare to get under the skin, travel through the guts, flex some muscles and whizz along the nerves as we learn about the human body.

This book is about human biology. That's the science behind what your body is made of and how all of its parts work – and why they are there in the first place.

Of course, you wouldn't be the first person to have wondered about what goes on under your skin. For thousands of years people have investigated the living machines that all of us call 'me.' They have sliced bodies open to have a look inside, zapped bits of limbs with electricity and peered up close with microscopes at blood, flesh and muscle. What they have found is an intricate collection of components: moving parts, control systems, fuel supplies and waste removers. There's even a section that can make things up or remind you about what it was like to be much younger (your mind).

One problem with this kind of dissection is that the patient had to be dead – or soon would be.

DON'T WORRY!
IT WON'T BITE.

I'M 100% ORGANIC

Like any complex machine, a body works on many levels. Our first chapter looks at basic stuff, from the cells that are the building blocks of the body to familiar features like hair and muscles. Next we consider the organs. These are hubs of activity that do the body's big jobs: the heart pumps blood, the stomach digests food, while the liver does a dozen things all at once. Then we look at the senses. These are the tools you use to listen to music, taste your food or read this book. The final chapter puts everything together into systems, where several parts team up. However you look at it, you'll find the human body pretty amazing – er, yes, even yours.

If you like a bit of blood and guts, you'll find them throughout this book, but especially on pages 26–27 and 46–47. If you are more fascinated by poo and pee then turn to pages 42–43 and 48–49. But if you find that a bit tiresome, find out about having a snooze on pages 90–91. Of course, we hope you are going to like it all. And that you find this book a breath of fresh air – especially pages 38–39.

I AM NOT TO YOUNG TO READ ABOUT POO!

DON'T BE SO TOUCHY!

MORE FUN THAN A DRAWING PIN IN THE BEHIND!

A BOX ON BOXES

Throughout this book you'll find different kinds of boxes. Under the Skin boxes take a detailed look at what's going on inside you. Yuck! boxes focus on the kind of thing you might prefer not to know about: the smelly, dirty or gross parts of the body (of course, this might be exactly what you DO want to know about). Superhuman boxes tell you about the individuals who helped discover exactly how the body works. Try This boxes have activities for you to try at home. None of them are dangerous: it's not exactly open-heart surgery. But use your common sense and ask an adult if you're not sure what you're doing.

WHAT'S INSIDE
A HUMAN BODY?

Your body is very complex, but it's actually created from simple chemicals, called elements, or from combinations of elements, called compounds.

Honestly, please don't try to break down your body. Really.

We don't really recommend anyone to break down their body into separate chemicals. It wouldn't be clever. But say it was possible (because you do realize that it's not, right?). You'd end up with a lot of piles – and a few surprises. For one thing, a lot of your body is made from stuff that turns up in all living things, such as carbon. For another thing, you might get a bit damp. The biggest single ingredient in your body is water.

WARNING
DON'T DISSOLVE

To make a 70 kg adult body you will need:

43 kg oxygen .... *used to make water*

16 kg carbon .... *needed for all organic chemicals*

7 kg hydrogen .... *water*

1.8 kg nitrogen .... *for the protein*

1 kg calcium .... *bones and teeth*

140 g potassium ... *used in muscles and nerves*

140 g sulphur ...... *for vitamins and enzymes*

100 g sodium .... *used in muscles and nerves*

95 g chlorine .... *used to transfer energy*

19 g magnesium ... *used in energy transfer*

6 g iron .... *used to transport oxygen*

Making a body

The human body is more than just a mixture of chemicals, otherwise you'd be able to make one in a laboratory. Of course, people have dreamed of doing just that for centuries. One of the most famous examples of making a human body is the story of Frankenstein. But Frankenstein cheated: he just stuck together bits of other bodies, then zapped his creature with lightning to bring it to life. Human biology doesn't work like that in reality. (In fact, it didn't work out very well for Frankenstein either. In the end, he got killed by the monster he created.) But Frankenstein was right about one thing. The human body depends on electrical sparks.

Frankenstein first appeared in a novel by Mary Shelley, published in 1818.

CALCIUM MAKES 206 BONES IN EVERY BODY

KETCHUP

PLUS
a sprinkling of copper, selenium, zinc, iodine and a dozen more trace elements that the body needs in tiny amounts.

Other stuff to do with what's inside a human body

- Make a 5-cm (2-inch) iron nail
- Make 900 graphite (carbon) pencils
- Make 2,000 matches from the phosphorus
- Kill the fleas on a dog with the sulphur
- Make enough gunpowder for one firework from the potassium, nitrogen and sulphur
- Fill 50 litre-bottles of water
- Sprinkle salt on 100 servings of chips
- Make a sparkler using the magnesium.

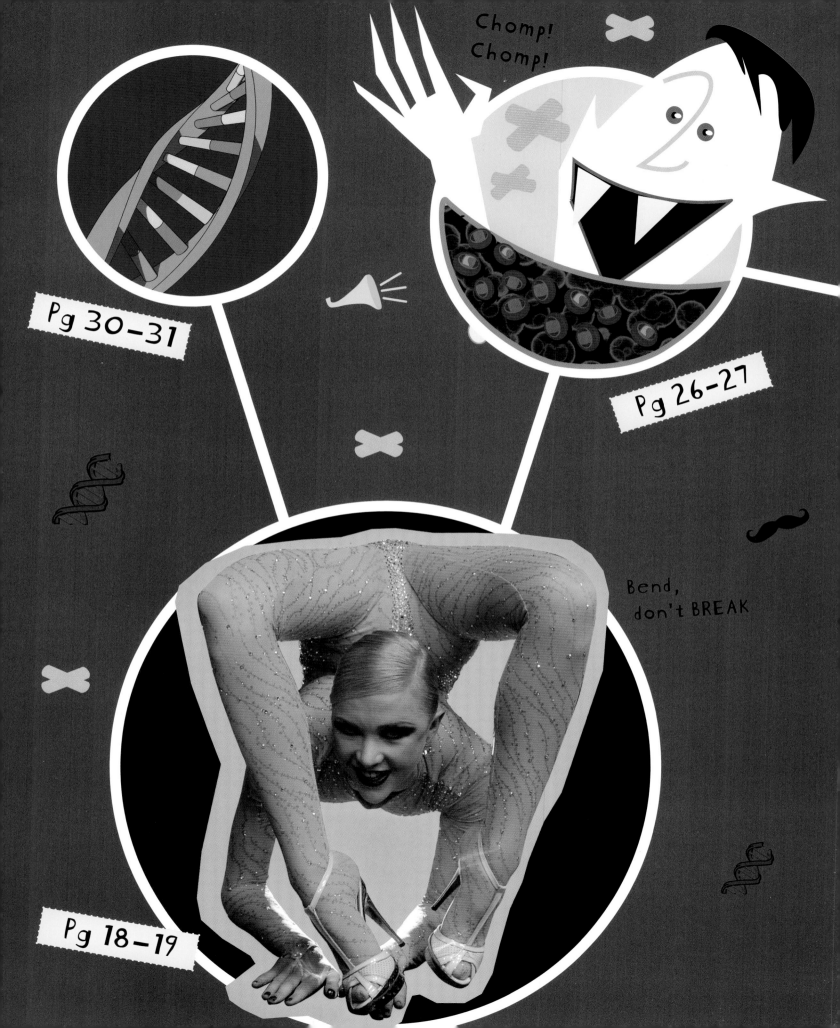

Pg 12-13

Too small to SEE!

THE BASICS

It might be hard to believe, but most of your body is made up of water. Of course, the body contains lots of other things, too. There are cells, which are the building blocks of the body. Then there are bones, muscles and joints. And there are special cells that decide whether a human will be a boy or a girl, and what he or she will inherit from his or her parents.

WARNING
MUSCLE POWER

big BICEPS

Pg 16-17

HELLO
EVERY BODY

What does a human body do? Its only real job is to keep working as long as possible. Think of it as a living machine, with a power supply, motors, sensors, control systems and exhaust pipes. So how is it different from non-living machines?

At first glance, you might think that it would be easy to tell a living body from a non-living machine. For example the body takes in fuel, sucks in air, moves around and expels waste. But then, so does a car.

One way to tell living from non-living is to consult Mrs Gren. She has a simple test of what to look for to show that something is alive: Movement, Respiration, Sensation, Growth, Reproduction, Excretion, Nutrition. That all adds up to MRS GREN.

Remember, non-living is not the same as dead. To be dead, you have to have been alive first.

While many machines can do some of these things – a car can move, a crystal can grow, while a high-tech factory robot could reproduce itself (by building another robot) – only living bodies do them all.

WARNING IT'S ALIVE!

M

Movement: There are several ways a body can move; humans do it by using muscles to lift and swivel levers of hard bone – better known as arms and legs (see pages 14–15 and 16–17).

S

Sensation: The body is aware of what is going on around it. Put simply, humans have five senses: sight, smell, taste, hearing and touch. The body is always checking and responding to what the senses detect.

R

Respiration: This is taking in oxygen from the air. Humans breathe it into our lungs (see pages 38–39), but other bodies use gills or take it in through the skin. The oxygen is used in cells to release energy, a process called cellular respiration, which is the second part of respiration.

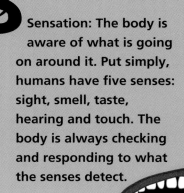

G Growth: Living bodies get bigger and repair themselves through growth. At its simplest, growth is one body cell dividing, making two new cells that are identical to each other.

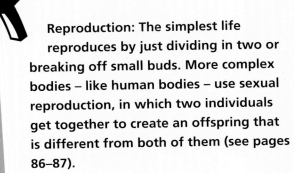

At the basis of all life is the cell. Meet the cells that make you human over the page.

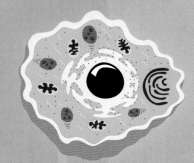

R Reproduction: The simplest life reproduces by just dividing in two or breaking off small buds. More complex bodies – like human bodies – use sexual reproduction, in which two individuals get together to create an offspring that is different from both of them (see pages 86–87).

E Excretion: This is the removal of waste. Humans excrete mainly by washing out waste in urine. (Pooing does not count as excretion.)

DANGER!

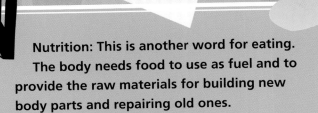

N Nutrition: This is another word for eating. The body needs food to use as fuel and to provide the raw materials for building new body parts and repairing old ones.

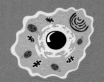

CONFINED TO THE CELLS

A human body is built up of units called cells. Almost all are way too small to see without a microscope, and an adult human has about 50 trillion of them! Cells are all built in the same way, but they can do different jobs.

Bacteria cells are hundreds of times smaller than a human cell, and they live inside and outside our bodies. Scientists estimate that there are 10 bacteria living on you for every cell of your own.

Most of a cell is a liquid called cytoplasm. That is largely water mixed with thousands of chemicals. The cell also contains dozens of small structures named organelles. It is these tiny machines that do the cell's hard work.

Every cell is surrounded by an outer covering, or membrane, made of two thin layers of fatty molecules called lipids. That creates a flexible bag that is just a few millionths of a centimetre thick – but thick enough to separate the inside of the cell from the outside world. Inside the cell, the work is done by folded packets of membrane called organelles. They're similar to the lipid layer that surrounds the cell. Different organelles have different functions – a bit like workers with different jobs in a factory.

SUPERHUMAN

ROBERT HOOKE

Living in Cells (1635–1703)
The first person to see a living cell was English scientist Robert Hooke. He built himself a microscope in the 1660s – back when it was a new invention – and used it to look at many living things. When he studied a piece of cork, a spongy material made from the bark of oak trees, Hooke saw that it was made up of thousands of tiny units. They reminded him of the little rooms that monks and nuns lived in, which were known as cells. (Back then prisoners were still kept in dungeons.) The building blocks of living bodies have been named cells ever since.

FACT

The cell membrane is peppered with proteins that run from one side to the other. These act as pores and pumps that allow chemicals to travel in and out of the cell.

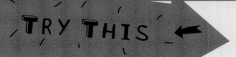

A BIT OF CHEEK

There's an easy way to see your own cells.

WHAT YOU'LL NEED

Microscope
Slide & cover slip
Eye dropper   Tissue
Food dye   Spoon
Toothpick   Water

Put a drop of water on the slide. Run a spoon along the inside of your cheek to collect some cheek cells. Use a toothpick to transfer the cells to the water. Gently lower the cover slip over the water. Put a tiny drop of food dye at one edge of the cover slip and use a tissue at the other edge to pull out the water and pull in the dye. Your cells are now ready to view: they will look like round bags with dark dots inside.

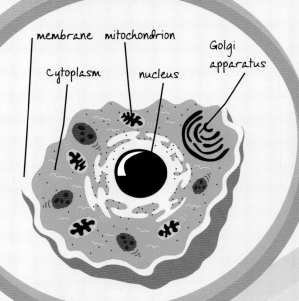

membrane   mitochondrion   Golgi apparatus

cytoplasm   nucleus

CELL FACTORIES

The organelles have different functions that turn cells into the factories of the body.

Nucleus: The largest organelle houses the genes. These are chemical codes that contain all the rules and regulations about how the cell is made and what it does.

Ribosomes: The job of these tiny dots is to translate the genetic code into specific proteins. Every cells uses thousands of different proteins in its toolkit.

Endoplasmic reticulum (ER): These twisting tubes of membrane act as the cell's transport network. Rough ER is so called because the tubes are studded with ribosomes: this is where most of the cell's proteins are made. Smooth ER makes lipids and other chemicals.

Golgi apparatus: This is a packaging plant for chemicals that are to be released from the cell. Substances are pack into membrane sacs, called vesicles, and hauled over to the cell membrane to be pushed out.

Lysosomes: These are the waste disposal unit of the cell. The lysosomes' job is to destroy waste, using powerful chemicals to break up large objects into simple materials that can be recycled.

Mitochondrion: The powerstation of the cell burns sugars to release the energy that keeps everything going.

PICK A BONE

No one likes being told to sit up straight – but be grateful that you can! Without bones, your body would be a floppy sack. You could not stand or walk. You'd have to wriggle on the ground and inch along like a human worm.

Giving shape

A body full of bones is known as a skeleton, and the human skeleton is made up of more than 200 bones. The skeleton provides the body's supports. The bones act like the columns and girders that hold up a building. Bones also protect the body's most vital parts. For example, the ribcage surrounds the heart, lungs and the other main organs, while the skull is a boney box for the brain. The skeleton is also a rigid frame to hang the muscles that allow the body to move.

Minerals are chemicals such as calcium that are vital for our health.

But that's only the start… The bones make the blood, they store important minerals and they are a holding centre for dangerous poisons before they can be be safely removed from the body. Oh, and without bones, we would not be able to hear (see page 62).

SUPERHUMAN

GALEN

Father of Anatomy (129–c.200/c.216)
For a thousand years the authority on the skeleton was Galen, a Roman doctor who looked after gladiators. However, it was illegal for Galen to study dead bodies, and he made many mistakes. The first accurate record of the skeleton comes from the 1540s, after the Flemish physician Andreas Vesalius stole dead bodies to study their anatomy.

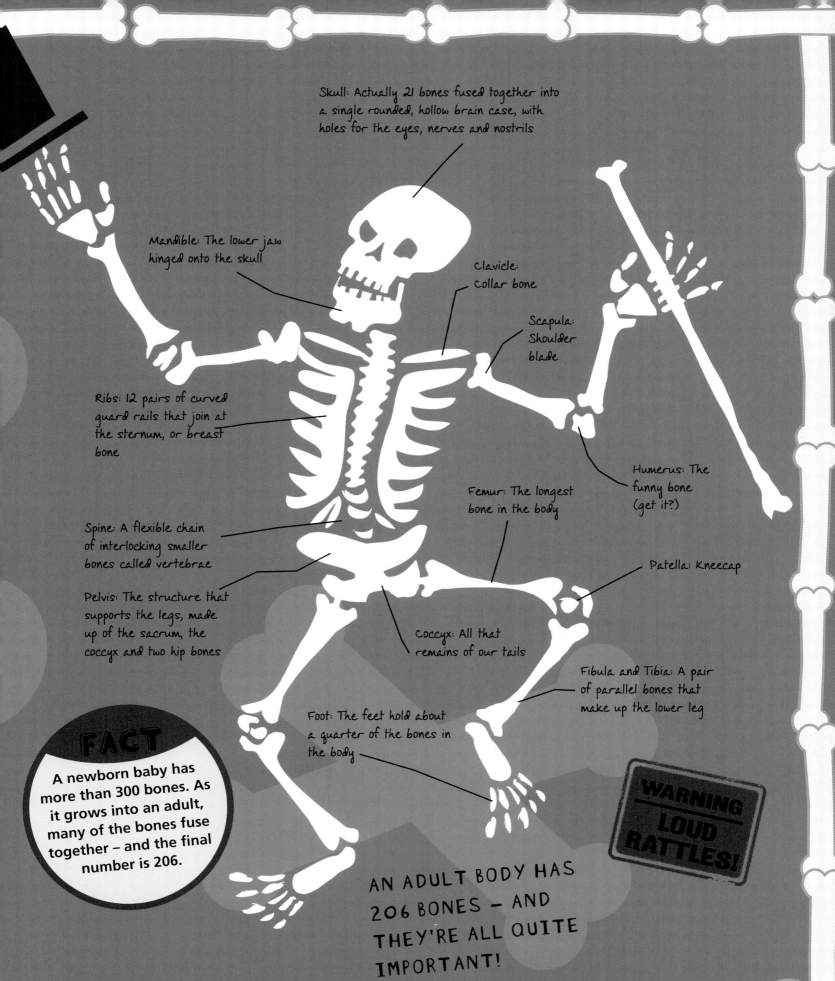

Skull: Actually 21 bones fused together into a single rounded, hollow brain case, with holes for the eyes, nerves and nostrils

Mandible: The lower jaw hinged onto the skull

Clavicle: Collar bone

Scapula: Shoulder blade

Ribs: 12 pairs of curved guard rails that join at the sternum, or breast bone

Humerus: The funny bone (get it?)

Femur: The longest bone in the body

Spine: A flexible chain of interlocking smaller bones called vertebrae

Patella: Kneecap

Pelvis: The structure that supports the legs, made up of the sacrum, the coccyx and two hip bones

Coccyx: All that remains of our tails

Fibula and Tibia: A pair of parallel bones that make up the lower leg

Foot: The feet hold about a quarter of the bones in the body

FACT

A newborn baby has more than 300 bones. As it grows into an adult, many of the bones fuse together – and the final number is 206.

WARNING
LOUD
RATTLES!

AN ADULT BODY HAS 206 BONES – AND THEY'RE ALL QUITE IMPORTANT!

MUSCLE BOUND

The fleshy part of the body is largely made from muscle. These are dense bundles of protein that can change their shape. They act as the body's lifters and shifters.

Show us your muscles! A muscle bulges when it is being used because all of the protein fibres inside have contracted, or shortened in length. That transforms the long slender slab of flesh into a short, thick one. When the muscle relaxes, it goes back to being long again.

The tough fibres that join muscles to bones are called tendons. Read more about them on pages 18–19.

Move it!

A muscle is normally (anchored) at one end to a bone. The other end may pull flesh into a new shape – such as if you smile or frown – or it may pull on another bone to make part of the body move. You have several hundred muscles. They work together to allow you to walk, wave, wink or whatever is the right movement at the time.

WARNING DON'T GET PUMPED!

Working in pairs

Millions of fibres combine to create a muscle's action. But muscles only pull; they never push. Most muscles work in pairs; one pulls in the opposite direction from its partner. When one contracts, the other relaxes.

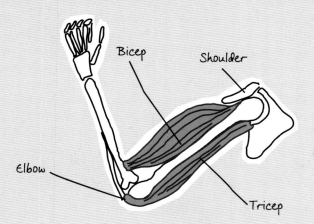

Bicep

Shoulder

Elbow

Tricep

SUPERHUMAN

LUIGI GALVANI

Electrical Biologist (1737–1798)

In 1771, Luigi Galvani found that electric sparks made the legs of freshly killed frogs twitch. Enough salty liquid still oozed through the flesh for the electricity to run along the muscles, making them contract. Galvani's discovery revealed how electricity moved in currents, and how it was used in living bodies. He put on shows of the amazing animal electricity. One person who took a great interest in his work was Mary Shelley, the author of *Frankenstein*!

Muscle types

The muscles used to move the body are called skeletal muscles. They are under our control – we can decide when they move, even though we leave them on autopilot for a lot of the time. However, we have no control over the second type of muscle. These are the smooth muscles that churn up the contents of your stomach, push blood through arteries (making your pulse) and even make your hairs stand on end.

The third kind of muscle is the strongest one of all. This is cardiac muscle, which is found only in the heart. It contracts to pump blood around the body dozens of times every minute for your entire life – without ever getting tired or needing to take a rest.

Under the Skin

Feel the Burn

After working hard, your muscles feel tired because they fill up with a burning acid. When the body cannot supply enough oxygen, a muscle takes energy from sugar in a different way. This results in lactic acid, which attacks and damages the muscle fibres. That's why you sometimes feel stiff for a few days as the muscles rebuild themselves after hard exercise.

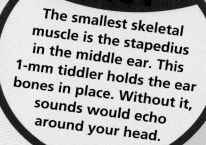

THE POINT OF JOINTS

Shoulder, elbow, ankle, knuckle, hip: many of our most familiar body parts are joints. These are the hinges and pivots around which the parts of the body swing and swivel. Joints work hard, so they're very hard wearing.

This toughness makes joints sturdy and supportive. But the hardness also causes problems. Two bones touching at a joint would rub and grind away at each other. To prevent this, the ends of the bones are cushioned with a spongy cartilage. In addition, both bone tips are surrounded by a bursa. This sac of thick gooey liquid – a bit like egg white – stops them knocking together.

Cartilage is a hard, bonelike substance. It makes up the skeletons of some fish, such as sharks.

Keeping it together

At a joint, the bones are joined by straps called ligaments. These connections are made from inflexible cartilage. They stop the joint from bending too far in the wrong direction. Ligaments stretch slowly, which is why athletes use stretches to lengthen their ligaments and get a wider range of movement. When you sprain a joint such as your ankle, you have overstretched its ligaments.

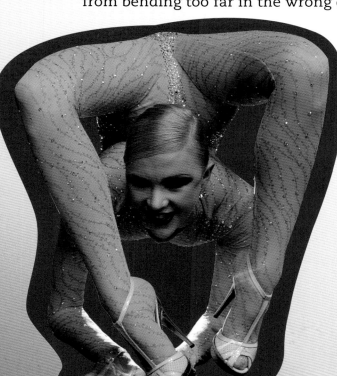

Power cable

Another kind of connector is called a tendon. Tendons join muscles to bones.

WARNING DON'T TWIST!

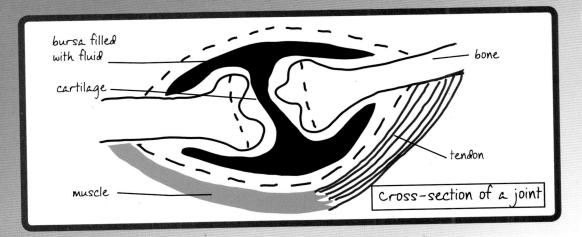

bursa filled with fluid

cartilage

bone

tendon

muscle

cross-section of a joint

As a muscle contracts, it pulls on the tendon; in turn, the tendon pulls the bone. Tendons cross joints, connecting a muscle on one side to a bone on the other. They transmit the muscle power that creates the movement.

Contrasting joints

Weightlifters and bodybuilders have short tendons: that leaves room around their joints to develop big muscles. In contrast, contortionists have stretchy ligaments that let them bend and twist. This hypermobility is often due to a fault with proteins in the ligaments, which leads to problems in later life.

TRY THIS

TENDON TEST

Are you flexible? Test the tendons in your hand.

WHAT YOU'LL NEED

A table
A hand (yours)

Place your hand palm down on a table, with the fingers spread out. Fold your fourth finger under to touch your palm. Now raise each finger off the table in turn, putting it down before lifting the next. Any problems? Uncurl the fourth finger and fold the middle finger under. Repeat the lifts. Try as you might, your fourth finger won't move. The tendon it shares with the middle finger is fully stretched. The muscle can't pull the tendon back to lift the fourth finger.

GIVE ME A HAND

You have a remarkable multi-tool made from 27 bones that can swivel, grip, poke and punch. One is located at the end of each arm. You call it a hand.

A HANDY GUIDE TO HANDS

The fingers and thumb work alone or as a team to do a wide range of jobs. The hand is one of the things that separates humans from animals. It allowed our ancestors to survive nearly anywhere – and it does the same today. Here are four ways how.

1 Hook
The four fingers can curl and lock into a hook to pull on heavy items.
Ancient: Pick up heavy rocks to find some damp earth.
Modern: Open the fridge door.

2 Grip
The fingers and palm wrap around an object, giving a powerful grip.
Ancient: Hold a stick to dig a hole to find water.
Modern: Take a bottle of water out of the fridge.

3 Pinch
A finger or two joins with the thumb to create a delicate grip.
Ancient: Pick a few juicy berries from a thorny shrub.
Modern: Take some sweets from a packet.

4 Wiggle
Each finger moves independently of the others.
Ancient: Daub a scene of a great hunt on a rock wall before going to sleep hoping for more food tomorrow.
Modern: Dial for a pizza.

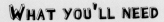
FINGERPRINTS
Check out your own unique pattern

WHAT YOU'LL NEED

A finger
Soft pencil
Deflated balloon

Rub a thick layer of pencil lead on a patch of paper (a soft 2B pencil works best). Press one fingertip onto the paper so it is covered in pencil lead. Carefully press that tip onto a deflated balloon. (You can do a few fingers per balloon.) Now blow up the balloon. You'll get a good view of the whirling lines that make up your unique fingerprints.

Remarkable digits

Doctors describe the fingers and thumbs – and the toes of the foot – as digits. We also use the same word for numbers, because people often learn to count by using their fingers.

Primates such as monkeys have opposable thumbs.

The whole human hand is remarkable, but its key component is the thumb. Unlike the other digits, the thumb is opposable. That means it can swing around in front of the palm and touch the tips of all the other fingers. This is what makes it possible for us to grip such a wide range of objects.

Structure

People crack their knuckles by displacing the joints, which causes a sound.

Each hand has 27 bones. The carpals form the wrist and give the hand its flexibility (you couldn't wave without them). The hand itself is made of long metacarpals, which lead to the digits. The four fingers each have three more bones called phalanges, joined by knuckles. The thumb only has two phalanges.

Touch sensitive

The fingers and palm are hairless and covered in fleshy folds of skin. The whole hand is very sensitive to touch. The fingertips have more pressure sensors than any other part of the body.

FACT

Every finger (and palm) print is unique. Even identical twins have different ones.

Under the Skin

Handedness

By the age of six months a baby starts to use one hand more than the other. Normally this is the right hand, but about 1 in 10 people are left handed. According to surveys, left handed people tend to be cleverer and richer – but that's not scientifically proven.

21

ALL THE TRIMMINGS

You never really stop growing. Even when your body reaches full size, you keep sprouting in all kinds of places. The most obvious (for most of us) is the hair on our heads, but we are covered in the stuff. What is it for?

Hair is not alive, which is why it does not hurt when we cut it. It is mostly made from a waxy, waterproof protein called keratin. Keratin is also found in the skin and is the stuff that makes fingernails. Keratin structures such as hair are tough – but they are not made to last. Hair would fall off the body, if we didn't trim it off first.

Keratin is also what makes horse hooves, bird feathers and animal claws.

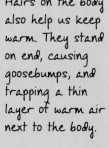

WARNING
GET A HAIRCUT!

Hairy head

Why do we have thick hair on our heads while the rest of the body is more thinly covered? No one really knows. The best suggestion is that it's to help us stay cool in strong sunlight but also to keep warm in cold places. Each hair shaft grows from a single root, or follicle, and sprouts over 1 cm every month. About 100 hairs fall out every day. But don't worry, they will grow back. And in any case, you have around 90,000 others on your head anyway.

Hairs on the body also help us keep warm. They stand on end, causing goosebumps, and trapping a thin layer of warm air next to the body.

Going bald

Several illnesses can cause people to lose their hair. In most cases, however, baldness is just part of growing up – and of being a man. Male-pattern baldness starts with hair thinning out on top of the head (the crown) or along the brow (or temple). The hair follicles just stop working. No one is sure why. Some bald men like to say it is because they have a lot of testosterone, the male hormone. That way, the balder they are, the more masculine they like to think they are. However, testosterone levels drop as men get older, but their baldness increases. So perhaps that isn't quite the explanation, after all.

Hair colour

The colour of hair depends on the levels of two pigments: eumelanin and pheomelanin. Eumelanin makes hair dark – black or brown – while red hair has mainly pheomelanin. Blonde hair has low levels of both pigments. Hair turns grey as the amount of pigment in it falls. White hair has no pigment at all.

SWEAT AND TEARS

Some hairs have special jobs. The eyebrows are like gutters for sweat from your forehead. The bushy brows direct it to the side, so it does not run into your eyes. Eyelashes, meanwhile, form a protective grill around your eyes, swatting away grit and bugs before they get too close. Armpit hair (the experts call it axilla) helps prevent rubbing when you swing your arms. It also pulls the sweat away from the skin, reducing smells and infections.

NUTS ABOUT NAILS

Instead of having sharp claws like other animals, humans have nails on their fingers and toes. The nails are made from keratin, like hair. They grow slowly – just over 3 cm a year – and make a hard upper surface for the tips of the digits, protecting the delicate fleshy underside. When you prod and poke things with the tip of a finger, the nail forms a solid ceiling that makes it easier to feel fine textures on the object's surface. Long nails are also useful for slicing and gouging food. Two nails together are perfect for gripping the tiniest of objects, such as a splinter in the skin.

FANGS A BUNCH

What body part is harder than gold, lasts for thousands of years – long after the rest of you has turned to dust – and is collected by fairies if you lose it?

Incisor: The sharp, slicing front teeth, used for taking the first bite. There are eight in all, located at the front of the mouth. If you smile, you'll see them. The upper incisor slide in front of the lower ones, cutting into food.

Teeth are food processors. They are built to slice, dice and then crush food into a gooey pulp that can slip down the throat easily. Without the teeth – and a gush of saliva – to soften things up, eating would be a very difficult job.

Most adults humans have 32 teeth, arranged top and bottom in sets of four. Not all teeth are the same. There are four types, each shaped to do a different job: incisors, canines, premolars and molars.

Milk teeth

Humans are born with no teeth. Teeth grow after six months or so. By about the age of two, babies have 20 teeth … but they will not last. These are the milk teeth. They are replaced by permanent teeth from the age of about seven onward. That's when the tooth fairy gets busy.

The tooth is coated in hard enamel that surrounds a soft pulp. The roots of the teeth are cemented firmly into the jawbone.

Canines: There are four of these fangs positioned along from the incisors. Unless you are a vampire, human canines are quite short but pointed. They grip tough food when you need to rip off a mouthful.

PIERRE FAUCHARD

Father of Dentistry (1678–1761)
Frenchman Fauchard invented the tooth drill, fillings and braces, and the dentist's chair. Dentists believed toothache was caused by worms in the teeth, until Fauchard realized that sugar was causing decay. But one of his innovations did not catch on: gargling with urine to keep the teeth healthy.

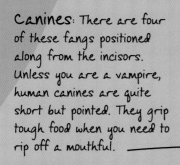

Premolar: Next to the canines are eight premolars. These flat teeth are used for grinding and crushing more than biting.

Don't lose your appetite

You know when pirates in movies bite on coins? They're testing if the coin is gold. Gold is soft (for a metal), so the teeth will leave a mark. The stuff that makes teeth so hard, enamel, is a mineral called hydroxyapatite – crystals made from calcium, phosphorus and oxygen.

Acids in food attack the enamel on the teeth, wearing it thinner. To protect the enamel, we rub toothpaste over the teeth to clean off the acids. Toothpastes often leave behind fluoride, which bonds to the crystals. When acids return after the next meal, they attack the fluoride instead, leaving the enamel as strong as ever.

Molar: At the back of the mouth are the molars. They look like large premolars and have more bumps for gripping food. The final molars arrive at around the age of 20, and so are called wisdom teeth. (Of course, some people never grow them.)

WARNING BRUSH OFTEN!

LIFE LIQUID

Don't faint! It's time to talk about blood, the thick liquid that oozes through your body – or out of it, if you are unlucky. Blood is the body's transport system. It takes oxygen and sugar fuel to every cell from your head to your toes. It does a lot more besides. In many ways, blood is liquid life.

The average human body contains about 5 litres of blood. That's not much, but without it you are in serious trouble. Blood's distinctive red colour is provided by iron-rich chemicals called haemoglobins. They make up the haulage system that ferries oxygen to the cells in the body. Blood also carries other essential chemicals: hormone messengers transmit commands to the organs (see page 34); immune system cells patrol for infecting invaders (see page 74); and repair crews are on standby to seal any breakages in the system.

5 litres is only about half of a household bucket.

FACT

The brown colour in poo is produced by the body getting rid of used-up haemoglobin from dead red blood cells.

ANTONI VAN LEEUWENHOEK

Microscope pioneer (1632–1723)

In 1674, the Dutch scientist Antoni van Leeuwenhoek used an early microscope to make the first drawing of red blood cells. He described them as corpuscles – the name is still used today. Van Leeuwenhoek estimated that each cell was about 25,000 times smaller than a grain of sand.

In the mix

Just under half the blood is made up of blood cells. Most are red blood cells, which are packed with haemoglobin. About 1 in 20 cells are so-called white blood cells. They control the immune system. The rest of the blood is a watery liquid known as plasma. Plasma contains hundreds of dissolved minerals, including waste carbon dioxide being taken to the lungs to be removed from the body (see page 38).

WARNING DON'T FAINT!

Sealing a hole

When there is break in the skin, blood rushes to fill the gap. The extra blood makes the area (swell) a little, closing the hole. The blood's repair system creates a solid patch, known as a clot or scab. Tiny cells called platelets give out a hormone that makes proteins in the plasma string together in a netlike solid called fibrin. Within minutes, this mesh has covered the hole to prevent infections getting in.

The blood also makes the area turn dark: we call it a bruise.

Receive from: Any
Give to: AB
AB

Receive from: A/O
Give to: A/AB
A

Receive from: B/O
Give to: B/AB
B

Receive from: O
Give to: Any
O

Under the Skin

Blood types

Everyone has a blood type, which is like an ID system for blood cells. There are four main groups: A, B , AB and O. The letters refer to markers, or antigens, on the cells. A and B are the two types of markers. AB cells have both markers, while O cells have none. It is essential that doctors know someone's blood type before a blood transfusion. Some blood types don't go together … at all.

GIRL-BOY:
WHAT'S THE DIFFERENCE?

You've probably noticed: girls' and boys' bodies are not quite the same. We all start off similar, but as we get older some big differences begin to show.

The differences between male and female bodies are called the sexual characteristics. Males tend to have certain features, while females have others. Scientists have a clever word for the differences: dichotomy. There is a good reason for sexual dichotomy. The female body is built to produce babies; while the male body is not.

Babies are born with either male or female genitals (see page 44) but that is the only difference. For the first few years, their bodies grow in the same way. But they start to develop differently at puberty. Puberty is the period when the human body transforms from that of a child into that of a fully functioning adult.

Female secondary sexual characteristics

FACE: The chin is rounded and face has very fine hairs.

BREASTS: The breasts grow rounded with fat tissue inside to be used as a source of baby milk after childbirth.

SKELETON: The hips are wider than the shoulders and the waist. The bones are narrower and muscles slender; joints are more flexible.

SKIN: The skin is smoother and softer due to thicker layers of fat underneath.

HANDS + FEET: Do not grow as large as a man's.

FACT
The longest beard ever grown belonged to Sarwan Singh of Canada. In 2010, it measured 2.37-m (7 ft 9 in) long. That was 1.5 times longer than his body.

Puberty processes

Puberty usually begins between the ages of about 10 and 12 and takes four or five years. It is started by hormones released by the sex organs. A boy's testes release the male hormone testosterone; while a girl's ovaries produce the female hormone oestrogen. These hormones turn on the sexual organs so they become capable of reproduction (see page 44). But puberty also produces secondary sexual characteristics that don't have a role in reproduction. They act as obvious signs of what a person's sex is, and show that he or she is sexually mature.

Male secondary sexual characteristics

HAIRINESS: Men have longer, thicker body hair than women, but head hair may become thinner as they get older.

FACE: The chin is square and covered in facial hair.

VOICE: The larynx enlarges, forming the 'Adam's apple'. This enables men to produce a wider range of sounds than women.

SKELETON: Bones are longer than in women, and muscles are thicker; the shoulders are wider than the waist.

SMELL: Men produce more skin oils and sweat – and can stink if they don't wash.

SKIN: The skin becomes rougher and has less soft fat underneath.

Under the Skin

Sex and gender

Two words describe the differences between male and female: sex and gender. They are not the same thing. The sexes are male and female; the genders are masculine and feminine. A person's sex relates to his or her anatomy. It is related to their chromosomes. A person's gender is about how he or she behaves. It is related to his or her culture. Gender can be complicated. Generally, males behave in a masculine way and females behave in a feminine way. But ideas of what 'masculine' and 'feminine' are vary. In a modern society, a person is usually allowed to choose how he or she lives.

Both sexes share some changes at puberty:

Underarm hair
Pubic hair
Deeper voice – although men's go much lower

GIVE ME A D, GIVE ME AN N, GIVE ME AN A

Making a human body is a complicated business. But with 255 new humans being born every minute, the system seems to work. The complexity is controlled by a chemical with a very simple name: DNA.

You can find out more about how genes shape the cells on pages 12–13.

The full name for DNA is deoxyribonucleic acid, so it's no wonder we shorten it. DNA occurs in the nucleus of every body cell (although some cells have lost their nucleus). It forms our genes, the 20,000 instructions needed to build all the different cells in a human body. DNA transmits the genes to us from our parents. Both parents give us a complete set of genes, so our cells actually have a unique double set of genes. That's what makes you you and not, er, someone else…

SUPERHUMAN

UNRAVELLING THE DNA

DNA was discovered in 1869, in pus oozing from wounds (yuck!). Scientists figured out that this stuff carried the genetic code, but no one could work out how. Then in 1953, James Watson and Francis Crick found the now famous double helix structure, which explained it all. They got a big clue about the structure from Photo 51, an X-ray photograph of the molecule taken by a researcher named Rosalind

EYES

OLD BLUE EYES IS BACK

A gene from Mum is different from one from Dad, and you have both in your DNA. Which do you use? Often one version of the gene is dominant over the other (which is described as recessive). For example, a gene for brown eyes is dominant over one for blue eyes. So a brown-eye gene from Dad and a blue-eye gene from Mum means you will have brown eyes. To end up with blue eyes, you need two versions of the recessive blue-eye gene. But it's still possible for you to have blue eyes, even if your parents both have brown eyes, if your Mum and Dad both have the recessive blue-eye gene.

Spiralling ladder

DNA is a polymer, a long molecule of millions of smaller units. DNA has two chains of deoxyribose molecules linked in a ladder. The sides of the ladder (the sugars) twist, forming a shape known as a double helix. The rungs are bases of nucleic acids that come in four types: adenine, thymine, guanine and cytosine, or ATGC for short.

Each rung is made up of a pair of bases. A is always linked to T and G to C. These bases create the genetic code, which is translated into proteins. The proteins are the building blocks of life. They are used for making everything else in the cell – and so in the whole body.

DNA is only 2.6 angstroms wide: that's about 2 billionths of a metre.

Keeping things neat

Every cell contains 3 metres of ultra-thin DNA. It's all coiled around a scaffold-like frame to make a chromosome, which is still too small to see with a microscope most of the time. A normal human cell has 46 chromosomes in the nucleus – 23 from Mum and 23 from Dad.

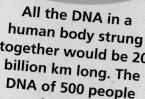

FACT

All the DNA in a human body strung together would be 20 billion km long. The DNA of 500 people would measure a lightyear!

MY HEART'S NOT REALLY IN THIS

Pp 34-35

Ahh-tennn-SHUN!

THE ORGANS

You know the phrase 'vital organs'? Well, it means what it says. The organs take care of the procedures that keep us alive. The lungs pass oxygen into the blood. The heart pumps blood around the body. The stomach digests food. The sex organs help us reproduce. The brain does our thinking. Most of the organs are in the torso, where they are protected by the rib cage. But not all your organs are inside you. Your largest organ is on the outside: your skin.

Pp 46-47

PLAYING THE ORGANS

There is no 'i' in cell, and no human cell can survive on its own. Body cells work as a team to achieve a common goal: staying alive. They need to get organ–ized!

Being a living, breathing human being is a complicated business, with trillions of cells, doing quadrillions of jobs all at the right time and in the right place. To get this right, the body uses layers of organization, or ranks. You can see the different levels like parts of a super-efficient army:

Organelles: kit bag
Cell: foot soldier
Tissue: platoon/squad
Organ: company
System: battalion
Body: regiment

- The cell is a foot soldier. Like a real soldier, a cell relies on the equipment in his kit bag: the organelles that power and process metabolism (see page 12).
- Cells that are specialized in the same jobs form a platoon, or a team, called a tissue. The cells in bones, nerves and muscles are examples of tissues.
- For the most important jobs, tissues band together to form organs. The body cannot survive without the so-called vital organs, such as the heart, lungs and liver.
- Organs and tissues are grouped into systems. For example, the circulatory system includes the heart, arteries and veins to transport blood around the body.

Tissue types

Body tissue falls into one of four types: muscular, connective, nervous and epithelial. Muscular tissues do the obvious: they move, shake and, er, apply muscle. Connective tissue includes bone and cartilage. It includes anything that holds the body together and protects the squidgier bits. (Blood is made in the bones, so it is classed as a connective tissue, too!). Nervous tissue can make you nervous, but also brave, and happy as well as sad. It makes up the body's messaging network. Finally, epithelial tissues cover the body's internal and external surfaces. They include the skin and stomach lining. These tissues often ooze out slimy chemicals, sometimes to protect the body.

Essential organs

Vital can mean 'full of life' but it also means 'essential'. The vital organs are both these things. They are the heart, lungs, liver, kidneys, pancreas and brain. We can just about do without some organs, such as the eyes, stomach or spleen – but it's not really recommended. But without lungs or a brain, life ends. The body takes no chances with these organs. The heart and lungs are packed in the chest and protected by a cage of ribs. The brain gets its own boney box (your skull, numbskull!).

The spleen is a small organ that helps keep red blood cells fresh.

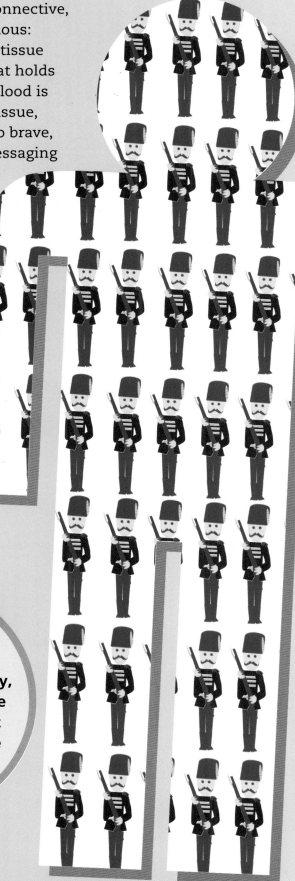

FACT

The smallest human organ is the pineal body, a pea-sized lump in the middle of the brain. It gets its name because it looks a little like a pine cone.

35

ALL HEART

You're all heart – really! When this fist-sized knot of muscle and pipes in the middle of your chest stops working, death is only seconds away. Yikes!

The heart is a blood pump. The 'buh-boom' sound of its beat is a clue to how it works. The organ is a ball of a special kind of muscle that never gets tired. It is divided into hollow chambers. Each half of the heart has an upper chamber – an atrium – and a lower one, called the ventricle. The first part of the heartbeat (the 'buh') is the atria contracting, squirting their contents into the ventricles beneath. The main 'boom' part of the heartbeat, a fraction of a second later, is the ventricles contracting. They are larger and more powerful. They push the blood out of the heart at high speed.

Get the rhythm

Your resting heart rate is a good indicator of your overall health.

An adult's heart beats once a second. Heart rate is a lot faster in children (a baby's is twice as fast), and it gradually slows down as they get older. To stay healthy, the heart needs to rest, and that means keeping fit. Smoking and eating fatty foods make the heart work too hard even when it is resting, so it will stop working sooner. One in three people die from an unhealthy heart.

TRY THIS

Rate your HEART RATE

(If you get a score of 0 or under, see a doctor!)

WHAT YOU'LL NEED

A watch with a second hand

Find your pulse: The best places are on the underside of the wrist, three finger widths below the thumb, or on the neck just below where your jawbone curves up into the skull. The pulse you feel is the surge of blood through a big artery as the heart beats, so it is a good way of counting your heartbeats. Count the number of pulses in 10 seconds and multiply by six to get the beats per minute (bpm). How does the bpm change straight after you've done 10 press ups? Wait 10 minutes more and count the pulses again. Is your heart rate higher or lower?

WILLIAM HARVEY

Heart monitor (1578–1657)

In the 17th-century doctors thought blood was made in the liver. Harvey worked out that, if this was true, the liver would have to make four times a person's weight in blood every day. Harvey cut into live animals. He worked out that the heart circulated blood from the lungs to the body and back again.

Left atrium receives blood from lungs and sends it to left ventricle

Right atrium receives blood from body and sends it to the right ventricle

FACT

It takes the heart less than a minute to pump all 5 litres of blood around the body once.

Left ventricle pumps oxygen-rich blood around the body

Right ventricle contracts and sends oxygen-poor blood to the lungs for more oxygen

39

TAKE A BREATH

And breathe... Oh, but you've been doing that all along. One crucial sign of life is the flow of air in through the mouth and nose and out again. The air passes through the lungs, two bags of flesh and blood that supply us with oxygen.

Air rushes into the body along a series of branching tubes. The main highway to the lungs is called the trachea, or windpipe. This thick-ribbed tube divides in the chest into two bronchi (one is called a bronchus), which each lead to a lung. The bronchi divide again and again into narrower tubes – named bronchioles. The tiny tubes extend every which way through the lung, so the fleshy sponge is more hollow than solid. The total length of all the tubes in a pair of lungs is 2,400 km – that's the distance from London to Athens.

Making the swap

Oxygen molecules like to be alone. When they are crowded together, the molecules spread into areas where there are less of them. This is called diffusion. It is how the lungs transfer oxygen from the air to the blood, and get rid of waste carbon dioxide the other way. The gas exchange takes place in clusters of tiny sacs, called alveoli, at the ends of every bronchiole. Air flows into each

Adult human lungs have about half a billion alveoli. If you flattened them out they would cover about 70 square metres, the same area as half a tennis court.

LONDON

ATHENS

THE LEFT LUNG IS SMALLER THAN THE RIGHT TO MAKE ROOM FOR THE HEART.

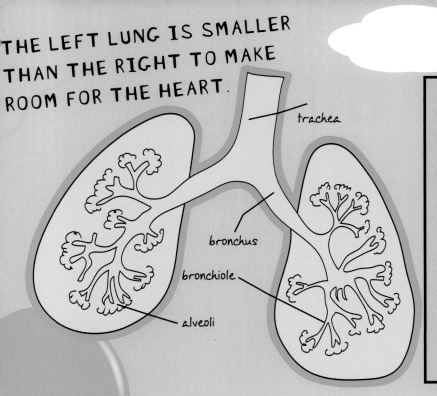

trachea

bronchus

bronchiole

alveoli

Acid Control

Imagine if you had to think about breathing. It would take up all your time (and if you went to sleep, you might die). Luckily for us, the body breathes automatically. Carbon dioxide dissolved in the blood creates acid; the more carbon dioxide there is, the more acidic the blood gets. That triggers the hypothalamus in the brain to tell the lungs to breathe faster, pumping out the waste gas and drawing in oxygenated air. When the body is inactive, like when we're asleep, it produces less carbon dioxide, so we breathe more slowly. If we're running around, we produce more carbon dioxide, so the brain automatically makes us breathe faster.

FACT

Champion cyclist Miguel Indurain's lung capacity was 7.6 litres – the average is just 6 litres.

alveolus, where the oxygen dissolves in a slimy coating around the edges. The alveolus is surrounded by a mesh of ultra-fine blood vessels full of blood that has run out of oxygen. As this blood pumps past, oxygen molecules from the lung diffuse through the walls of the alveolus and are picked up by haemoglobin molecules in the blood. At the same time, carbon dioxide passes from the blood into the alveolus. It is cleared out of the lungs and pumped out of the body as we breathe out.

Life under pressure

To breathe in, or inhale, a curved sheet of muscle under the lungs – the diaphragm – contracts and flattens. Muscles pull the ribs sideways. These movements expand the lungs, and air rushes in. To exhale (breathe out), you relax the same muscle. The lungs collapse a little, which squeezes out the air inside them. (If your rib muscles and diaphragm aren't working as a team, they create jerky breaths – and cause hiccups.)

DURING EXERCISE, THE LUNGS FILL MORE DEEPLY.

LIFE OF A LIVER

If the heart is the romantic hero of the body, and the brain is the clever one, the liver is the trusty assistant that does the hard work behind the scenes.

The liver has dozens of jobs on its to-do list ... and it is built for hard work. It is the largest organ in the body. The liver is slightly heavier than the dense brain upstairs and almost twice its size. On the outside it looks like a shiny brown blob, divided into four unequal sections, or lobes. Inside, the liver is busy being the body's storage depot, recycling centre, food distribution hub and chemical plant all rolled into one.

Portal vein

The liver's blood supply is a clue to what it does. Every other organ is fed by arteries carrying blood brimming with oxygen-rich blood fresh from the lungs. The liver, on the other hand, gets most of its blood from a thick vein that arrives from the small intestine. This hepatic portal vein contains all the nutrients that the digestive system has managed to remove from whatever you've eaten, and it must go to the liver before feeding the rest of the body.

Hepatic means 'connected to the liver'.

SWOOSH
SWIS

FACT

If your liver is not working properly, your eyes will turn yellow.

Building up...

The liver gets first dibs on all those useful chemical building blocks so it can make many of the most essential substances needed by the body, like fibrin and energy. The liver also makes cholesterol. This fatty material has a bad name, because if you are overweight, the extra cholesterol damages the heart. But cholesterol does a vital job in the cells. Without it, life could never have evolved beyond titchy bacteria.

...breaking down

The liver is also a wrecker's yard. It smashes up the old stuff that the body does not need any more. The liver breaks down dead red blood cells; it takes out the toxic nitrogen from unwanted proteins, making the urea that ends up in urine (see page 42); and it also creates bile. This green slimy mixture of acids is funnelled through the gall bladder into the intestines, where it attacks oils and fats in food to help the digestion (see page 80).

FIBRIN
The liver makes the proteins the blood uses to form clots to stop cuts from bleeding.

CHOLESTEROL
The liver produces cholesterol to make the membranes that surround the cells.

ENERGY
The liver uses glucose and other sugars from the gut to set up stores of energy.

BILE
The liver makes this fluid to help with digestion.

WARNING LIVING LIVER

Under the Skin

Prometheus: Regeneration

According to a Greek myth, people learned how to use fire when Prometheus stole it from the gods. The gods punished him by tying him to a rock. Every day, an eagle visited and pecked out his liver. Overnight Prometheus's liver grew back, and he went through the same agony again the next day – for ever! Although this is just a story, the liver really can regenerate. Doctors transplant small pieces of liver into patients, where they grow to full size. No other organ can regenerate like this.

PEE PROCEDURE

Experts call it excretion, but the rest of us call it having a pee. The human body flushes out waste and any other nasties in liquid urine.

Even the healthiest body is full of toxins. These poisonous chemicals could cause illness or even kill you. But don't panic. You haven't been poisoned. These toxins are all natural and are easily controlled. We get rid of them when we have a pee.

Yucky urea

One of the worst offending (toxins) is urea. This is a nitrogen-containing chemical that is produced when we digest proteins. (Meat-based food has the most protein in it, but the proteins in vegetarian food are just the same.) Urea and other unwanted chemicals build up in the blood until they arrive at one of your two kidneys. Imagine a kidney bean (they got their name for a reason) big enough to fill the palm of your hand. You have two kidneys, located on either side of the small of your back.

Most toxins are produced naturally by various functions of the body. They're harmless, as long as they don't build up in large quantities.

SUPERHUMAN

FRIEDRICH WÖHLER

Your Urea User (1800–1882)
People used to believe that chemicals in living things – organic chemicals – were different from chemicals made in a laboratory. Then in 1828, the German chemist Friedrich Wöhler made some urea by accident. (He was trying to produce something else.) Wöhler showed that organic chemicals were just like ordinary chemicals in the way they behaved.

Filter system

Each kidney has about one million filtration units called nephrons. Blood is delivered to each nephron in ultrafine capillaries. These have such thin walls that the liquid parts of the blood (where all the nasty stuff is) leak out. The liquid is collected in a cup-shaped capsule connected to a long tube. As it passes along the tube, any useful chemicals like salts and water are taken out and returned to the blood. The rest trickles into a funnel in the middle of the kidney and from there down a tube called the ureter to the bladder.

Time to go

The bladder is a stretching bag. An adult's bladder could hold almost a litre of urine but we usually get the urge to 'go' when it holds about 300 ml. The urine presses down on an opening closed tight by a couple of circular muscles, or sphincters. When we relax this opening, the liquid flows under the force of gravity (no need to push!) along a tube called the urethra, out of the body ... and hopefully into a lavatory!

Under the Skin

The ADH game

One job of the kidneys is to control the amount of water in the body. If there is too much, you pee to get rid of the extra. The process is controlled by ADH, a hormone. A gland called the pituitary releases ADH when your body is low on water. That makes the kidney return more water to the blood. Soon there is too much water in the blood, so the ADH drops. The nephrons stop absorbing water, and it is time for another pee.

43

THE UNMENTIONABLES: SEX ORGANS

There's no need to be embarrassed: we all have sex organs. Their main role is to produce sex cells – sperms and eggs – that join together to form a new human. However, the body also uses them for weeing out urine.

There are many names for the human sex organs. You might know quite a lot of them. Most are a bit silly. But there is nothing silly about these organs. Without them, none of us would be here. The sex organs, or genitals, are located in the (pelvis,) between the hips. Male and female genitals have several different components, but their biological purpose is to allow men and women to have sex. Both male and female organs produce sex cells, called gametes. When a male and a female gamete join, they produce a brand new human.

The pelvis is shaped differently in men and women, to allow women to give birth more easily.

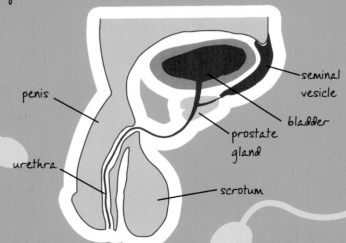

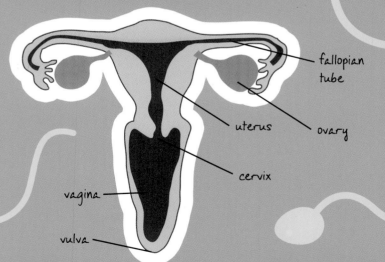

penis
seminal vesicle
bladder
prostate gland
urethra
scrotum

fallopian tube
uterus
ovary
cervix
vagina
vulva

MALE SYSTEM

Male gametes – sperms – are made in two testes. These dangle outside the main part of the body in a fleshy bag called the scrotum. The sperm travels along a series of tubes, being mixed with water and chemicals along the way to create a milky liquid called semen. Semen leaves the body through the penis via the urethra, a tube that runs down the middle of the penis and is also used for peeing.

FEMALE SYSTEM

Female gametes – eggs – are produced in two ovaries. Eggs are carried from each ovary along a tube to a central uterus or womb. This is where a baby develops. The uterus is connected by a muscular seal called the cervix to the vagina. The urethra, a tube that drains urine from the bladder, joins the opening of the vagina at the vulva, so this is where females pee as well.

WIGGLE!

WIGGLE!

The bit about sex

To create new life, a man's sperm cell needs to fuse with a woman's egg. This process, known as conception, takes place inside one of the woman's fallopian tubes. As the egg travels to the uterus, it meets a sperm coming the other way. How did it get there? The answer is sexual intercourse, in which the man inserts his penis into the woman's vagina. Semen is pumped out of the penis onto the cervix. The millions of sperms in it then wriggle through a tiny opening into the uterus and race to the egg. If a sperm and egg meet in the right place at the right time, they fuse together and create a new cell called a zygote. This is the first cell of a new human. The woman is pregnant! A baby will grow inside her for nine months – but it will need care and attention for many more years after it is born.

Preparing the way

The male testes produce sperm all the time, but the female ovaries only release one egg every four or five weeks. That's because the uterus needs to provide the right environment for a growing baby. It runs on a cycle in which the lining of the uterus thickens ready for the arrival of an egg. If no pregnancy occurs, the lining is shed through the vagina. This causes a few days of bleeding known as the menstrual period. That clears the uterus so it can prepare for the next egg.

Under the Skin

Big and small

What's the difference between an egg and sperm? A sperm's only job is to reach an egg. It is a streamlined swimming machine, using a tail-like flagellum to race through the uterus. The winner hands over a half-set of genes to the egg (see pages 86–87) – and that's him done. The egg provides the other half-set of genes … and everything else! Her job is just beginning, because she must provide all the energy and cell equipment needed for the new life to grow.

DIGESTION ENGINE

Whatever anyone says, we all have a strong stomach. The stomach converts everything you eat into mush in a matter of minutes.

The stomach is like your own personal food mixer. The difference is that, instead of whizzing and whipping ingredients together to make something tasty, this muscly bag is busy breaking them apart.

The oesophagus is sometimes called the gullet. It's a tube that joins the pharynx at the back of the mouth to the stomach.

Everything arrives in the stomach as a gooey mush that slides down the oesophagus. The food is let into the stomach by a valve that closes behind it – which is just as well. The lining of the stomach secretes a powerful acid that attacks the food, breaking it into smaller components. The stomach lining is protected from the acid by a layer of mucus. But if acid leaks out, it burns the oesophagus. The pain is known as indigestion.

FACT

The stomach expands as it fills with food. When it's empty, the stomach is not much bigger than your clenched fist. After a big meal, it can swell to 10 times that size.

After a meal, blood is diverted to the stomach while it does its job. If you are active too soon after a meal, your muscles use up most of the blood's oxygen. If your stomach runs out of oxygen, it gives out a sharp ache. That ache is called a stitch. The best way to get rid of a stitch is to breathe deeply and steadily, and to blow out hard between in-breaths.

FACT

Stomach acid is strong enough to dissolve steel (although only very slowly).

Once the stomach is full of food, it sends a message to tell the brain to stop feeling hungry. The stomach's muscular walls squeeze the food and grind it around. The food breaks apart and mixes with the acid and other digestive chemicals that split the complex ingredients into simple ones. Over three hours or so, all the solid food is turned to a liquid. The liquid leaves the stomach by a back entrance that leads to the intestines. This is where the body will picks the items it wants before getting rid of the leftovers.

TRY THIS

Make an EXTRA STOMACH

(Looking inside your own stomach could be tricky.)

WHAT YOU'LL NEED
Large ziplock bag
Half a cup of fizzy drink (or lemon juice)
Half a slice of bread (white works best)

See for yourself how the stomach works with this simple experiment. The bag plays the part of the stomach, and the drink is the acidic stomach juice. The bread is appearing as itself – some bread.

Pour the liquid into the bag and drop in the bread. Make sure the bag is securely zipped and then give it a shake and squeeze for about a minute. Once you are done, the bread will have been been digested into a mushy starch soup. The real stomach does the same. The acid breaks up solid food into liquid ready for processing by the intestines.

THE BOTTOM END

You have several metres of tubes twisting and turning through your abdomen. These are the intestines. They are processors that absorb all the goodness from the food you eat and then package up the leftovers as solid waste.

You have two intestines: the large intestine and the small intestine. The small intestine is actually bigger than the large one. But there is a logic behind the names, sort of. The small intestine is a tube connected to the base of the stomach. It is about 6 metres long, but it is only about 3-cm across (that's why it's called 'small'). The large intestine comes next; it is only 1.5 metres long, but it is much wider than its 'small' equivalent (that's why it's called 'large').

WARNING! A BIT GROSS!

POO PATROL

If you want to know about poo, the large intestine is the place to go. Food waste ends up here after the nutrients have been removed in the small intestine. The job of the large intestine is to remove all the water and produce a solid stool – that's what doctors call poo. The large intestine starts quite near the bottom, but the food waste makes a complete loop up and over inside the body before it is expelled. Eventually it reaches the rectum. This compaction chamber shapes poo ready for shipping out. As the rectum fills up, a signal goes to the brain: 'It's time to go.' The large intestine ends at the anus, a muscular valve. When the anus is relaxed, the rectum contracts, pushing poo out of the opening.

USELESS DEAD END

The French surgeon Claudius Aymand is famous for cutting out a tiny branch of the large intestine called the appendix. No one is sure what the appendix is for. It may be a gut section that humans no longer need, or it may store bacteria to help to keep our bowels healthy. The appendix can get clogged up or infected. If it bursts, the only thing to do is cut it out. Aymand performed the first appendectomy (appendix removal) in 1736. He saved the life of an 11-year-old boy.

Intense intestine

Smooth muscles work without you having to control them at all.

The small intestine is where most of the nutrients released by digestion are taken into the blood. The tube has smooth muscle on the outside to push food along it. The inner lining is uneven and tightly folded. This makes its surface area as large as possible. Each fold is covered in hair-like projections called villi, and every villi is covered in microvilli. All that area exists to take in nutrients from the liquid food passing through the intestine. Sugars and amino acids (protein units) cross the lining straight into the blood. Fats go into a lymphatic vessel (see page 74). They drip into a much larger vein near the heart.

FACT

The intestines are roughly five times as long as a person's body. An adult woman's intestines are normally slightly longer than a man's.

TRY THIS

LISTEN TO YOUR TUMMY

Prepare for something horrible: the noises of your insides

WHAT YOU'LL NEED

A stomach
2 plastic funnels
Flexible tube
(or a stethoscope)

A stethoscope is not just for listening to the heart: you can hear your intestines, too. If you are not a doctor, you can make your own stethoscope. You can do this by taping a small plastic funnel to each end of a flexible tube. (Rolled up card or paper works just as well, but you can only listen to someone else with it, not yourself.) Put one end on your stomach and the other to your ear. What can you hear?

GIVING VOICE

Ahem, it's time we talked about talking. The human voice is formed by flaps of skin that reshape our air passages – and by an uncanny ability to stop breathing.

Clearing your throat before speaking is a good idea, because the throat is where it all happens. The voice box – properly known as the larynx – is a section of the windpipe that is thickened with cartilage. Any air coming in or out of the body passes through it, but you only speak when you're breathing out. (Try it for yourself. Trying to talk when you're breathing in only makes a rasping, gasping noise.)

Cartilage is an elastic but very tough substance that forms many of the body's joints.

Flaps and levers

The sounds we use to speak are a series of waves travelling through the air. The larynx creates those waves and shapes them into the many different sounds we produce. As air rushes up through the larynx, two flaps of skin close over the throat using a complex system of cartilage levers. These flaps are called the vocal cords. They form a small, changing gap for the air to pass through.

FACT

We all really do speak from our hearts. The muscles in the voice box are controlled by the same nerves that keep the heart beating.

Lower your voice

The human larynx does not stay in one place. A baby's larynx is high up near its nose, making it easier for the baby to breathe and eat – and cry. But as we get older and bigger, the larynx shifts its position down the throat. This makes it easier for us to speak clearly. It also means that adults have deeper voices than children. A teenage boy's voice 'breaks', or becomes deeper, as his larynx gets larger. The larynx forms the 'Adam's apple' in a boy's throat (girls don't have an Adam's apple).

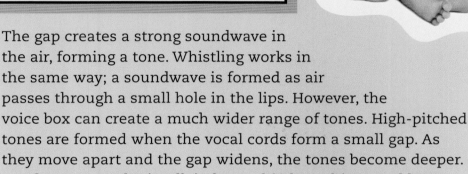

The gap creates a strong soundwave in the air, forming a tone. Whistling works in the same way; a soundwave is formed as air passes through a small hole in the lips. However, the voice box can create a much wider range of tones. High-pitched tones are formed when the vocal cords form a small gap. As they move apart and the gap widens, the tones become deeper.

Of course we don't talk in long whistles, whines and hums. Instead, as babies learn to talk, they train their voice boxes to make a series of short sounds. They learn to alter those sounds with their tongue, lips and teeth to form different words.

Fish, fish and, er, more fish

Learning to talk takes a human baby about two years.

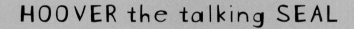

HOOVER the talking SEAL

Why do only humans talk when other animals only hoot, howl and roar? There is one key thing humans can do that most other animals cannot: stop breathing. Without this ability we would have to string words together or only say one word per breath. Most animals cannot control their breath. An exception is sea mammals, such as seals, which hold their breath underwater. In the 1970s and 1980s, a seal called Hoover (he sucked up food, geddit?!) lived in an aquarium in Boston, USA. Hoover learned to say a few words, because he could control his breathing. His favourite phrase was 'Get outta here!'

THE SKIN YOU'RE IN

The largest body organ is the only one you can see and touch. It's the skin. And it does a lot more than just cover the body.

Imagine a material that is strong but flexible, waterproof, mends any rips, cools itself down or heats itself up – and renews itself every month. Just think how useful it would be. Well, you're wearing some right now. It's your birthday suit, or your skin.

Waterproof coating

The skin has three layers. The top layer is the bit we can see, which is called the epidermis. It's made from stacks of dead cells coated in keratin. This waxy protein is the same stuff that forms your hair and fingernails. Its job is to make the skin waterproof. As the skin rubs and bumps on objects, the dead cells fall away, so the skin doesn't get damaged. It takes about four weeks for the skin to shed the entire outer layer (that's why a sun tan doesn't last long).

Keratin cells bundle together to form filaments, which harden into hair and become even harder to form nails.

Under the Skin

Pigmentation

You don't have to look far to see that skin comes in many different colours. This pigmentation is mainly produced by a substance called melanin in the epidermis. (It doesn't even reach the dermis, so colour isn't even skin deep!) The main purpose of melanin is to protect the skin from harmful ultraviolet rays in sunlight. Darker skin has more melanin, and so is better protected from the sun. Lighter skin tends to burn more easily.

52

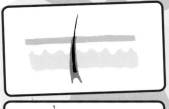

Three-ply TISSUE

- The skin is formed from a triple layer of tissues.
- The upper layer is the epidermis. Its job is to waterproof the skin and protect it from damage.
- The middle layer is called the dermis. This network of fibres gives the skin its strength and flexibility. The dermis contains the skin's sweat glands and touch detectors.
- The lower layer is fat. It's there to provide a soft cushion and keep the upper layers supplied with the moisture and nutrients.

The thickness of the skin varies. Around the eyes, it is only 0.5-mm thick, so it can be pulled tight around the eye sockets. The skin on the soles of the feet, however, is almost 10 times as thick because it needs to be very tough. If an area of skin gets worn away regularly, the skin forms thick calluses.

Temperature control

To keep warm, the skin uses hairs. Most skin is covered in short hairs. On cold days, a tiny muscle pulls each hair upright to trap a blanket of air, keeping the body a little warmer. This is what happens when we get goosebumps. To cool down, glands in the dermis pump out droplets of salty water, better known as sweat. As this water evaporates, it takes some of the heat from the skin.

FACT

Each square centimetre of human skin contains one metre of blood vessels.

Sealing a hole

If there is a break in the skin – a cut – blood rushes to the area, filling the gap. The extra blood makes the area swell a little, helping to push the hole closed. The damage triggers the repair system in the blood to create a solid patch, known as a clot or a scab. Clotting is controlled by tiny blood cells called platelets. The platelets release a hormone that makes proteins in blood plasma string together to make a mesh called fibrin. Within minutes, the fibrin has covered the hole to prevent infections getting in while the epidermis is replaced underneath. If the cut is deep enough to go into the dermis layer, a scar forms where the collagen fibres have reconnected.

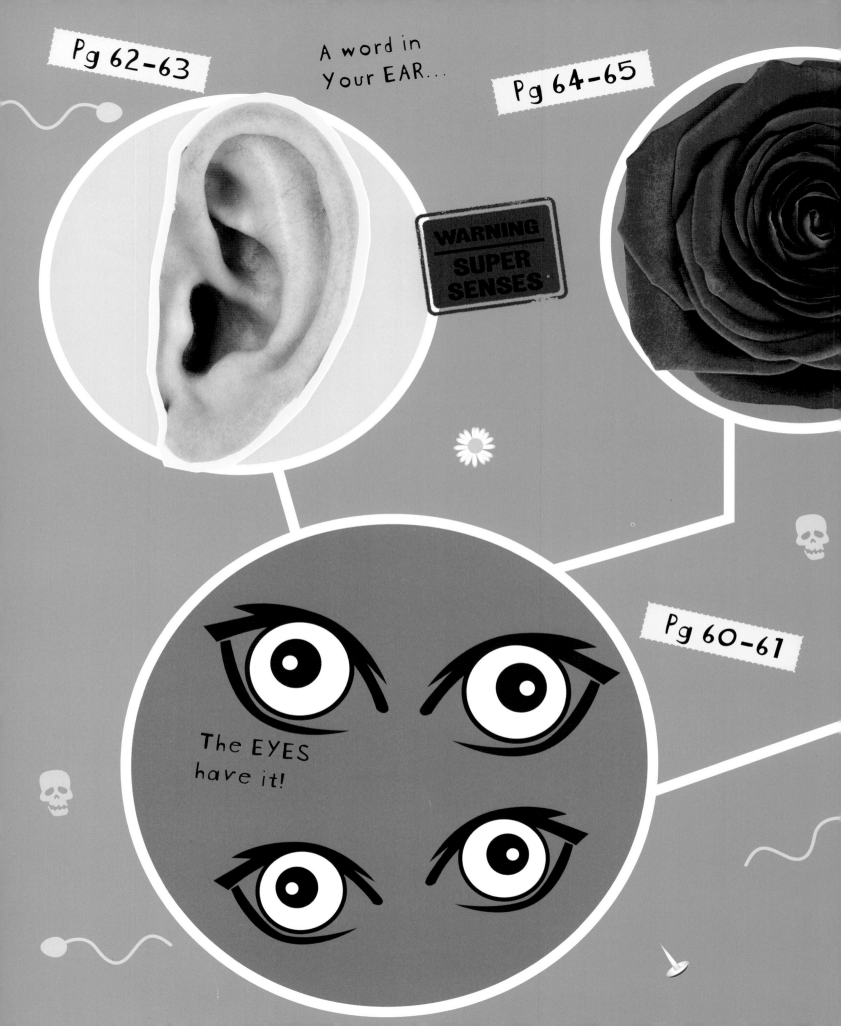

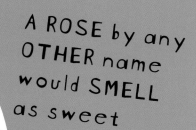

A ROSE by any OTHER name would SMELL as sweet

Pg 66–67

It's on the TIP of my tongue

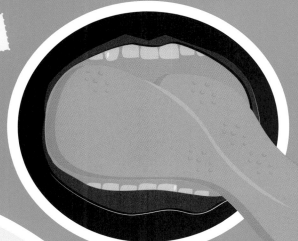

THE SENSES

This chapter is all about how you experience the world around you. The body has many different ways to receive information about what is around it. It's useful for being able to avoid danger, find food and communicate with others. We receive signals about the world from our senses: touch, sight, taste, smell and hearing. The body processes the information in the most powerful supercomputer in the world: the human brain.

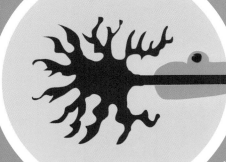

Pg 58–59

YOU'RE A BRAINBOX

The brain is the boss of the body. If the brain doesn't work, the body has no future. But just how does this ball of fat and water create a headful of thoughts and deeds?

Have you heard the phrase 'nerve centre'? It could be a control room where technicians run a space mission or a military headquarters where generals send out orders. But the best nerve centre is the human brain. All the nerves in the body end up there.

Cell network

The brain is a mass of nerve cells called neurons: 100 billion neurons, to be not-very-precise, in a full-sized brain. Each neuron is connected to hundreds of its neighbours, creating a network a million times more complicated than the whole of the Internet. The way the brain is wired up is mind-boggling. The human brain is not clever enough to understand how it all connects. But some clever people are working on it!

You can read more about nerve cells on pages 58–59.

You can read more about nerve cells on pages 58–59.

FACT
The brain makes up just 2 percent of the weight of the body but uses 20 percent of its energy.

SUPERHUMAN

HANS BERGER

Hans Has a Brain Wave (1873–1941)
The brain's cells are always sending and receiving electric pulses. Added together, these sparks form an electrical field around the head that can be picked up by sensors. In 1924, a German doctor called Hans Berger recorded how the force field changed. He was the first person to measure what became known as brain waves. He used a machine called electroencephalograph or EEG (it means 'electric brain measurer'). EEGs show how our brain waves change, depending on what we are doing.

Command structure

One set of nerves, called sensory neurons, bring reports from the senses to tell the brain what is going on. The brain then sends out commands to muscles and organs through another set of nerves, called the motor neurons.

Bigger animals have bigger brains than ours. A blue whale's brain is four times bigger, for example – but its body is 2,500 times larger. Compared to body size, the human brain is by far the biggest. That is because of its huge cerebrum, which does the thinking and feeling. It makes up three quarters of the brain, and folds in on itself to make room for neurons.

Brain box

The brain is well protected. On the outside is the skull, which is made from several bones fused into a solid case. Inside the skull, the brain is cushioned by an inner layer of thick liquid, called cerebrospinal fluid. This liquid stops the brain moving around inside the head and banging against the skull.

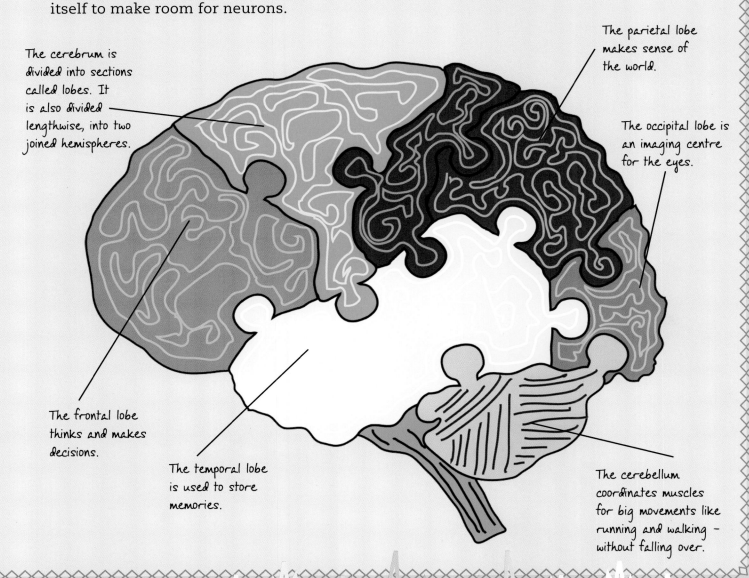

The cerebrum is divided into sections called lobes. It is also divided lengthwise, into two joined hemispheres.

The parietal lobe makes sense of the world.

The occipital lobe is an imaging centre for the eyes.

The frontal lobe thinks and makes decisions.

The temporal lobe is used to store memories.

The cerebellum coordinates muscles for big movements like running and walking – without falling over.

ON THE NERVES

Don't worry, you don't need to be nervous about the nervous system. It is the communication network of the body, collecting information and carrying messages.

The eyes do not see, the ears do not hear, the nose doesn't smell and the skin does not feel. Everything we sense is created by the brain based on information received from the sense organs. That information is taken to the brain by the nerves – and only then do we know about it. We only react once other nerves carry commands to muscles or other body parts.

Branching out

The nervous system is an electrical network. The nerve cells, or neurons, form long wires that carry signals as pulses of electricity. Neurons are the longest cells in the body: a single cell runs from the base of the spine to the big toe. Dozens of narrow branches extend from the cell body. The longest, thickest one is called the axon. It carries signals to the next cell in the system. The shorter branches are dendrites, which receive signals from the axons of neighbouring nerve cells. In the brain, a neuron can have hundreds of dendrites.

BRIGHT SPARK!

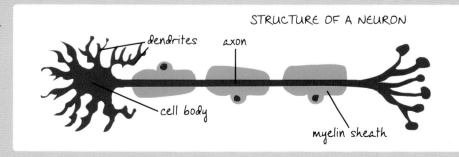

STRUCTURE OF A NEURON

dendrites
axon
cell body
myelin sheath

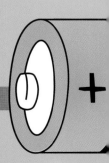

Under the Skin

Mind the gap

Neurons do not have electrical connections. Next-door cells do not touch each other at all. There is a tiny gap between the tip of one cell's axon and the next cell's dendrite. The distance is a few millionths of a millimetre, and signals are sent across as special chemicals called neurotransmitters. These are released through the axon's membrane when it becomes electrified by a nerve signal. They flood over the gap and stick to the membrane of the dendrite. That kick starts another surge of charge, and off the signal goes again.

Making a difference

Electricity occurs when there is a difference in charge. If one area of a system is positive and another is negative, charge flows between them to even it out. Nerves do not actually have an electric current running through them, but they use a difference in charges in a different way. The inside of the neuron has a negative charge and the outside is positive.

When the neuron fires, gates in the axon's membrane open, and the positive particles (called ions) flood inside, changing the charge difference to positive inside and negative outside. This happens for a fraction of a second, and causes the same process to start a little further along the axon. A spike of charge surges all the way along the axon, creating a nerve signal. Job done. Just like an electric cable's plastic cover, the longest nerves have an insulating coating. Instead of plastic, it is a fat layer called myelin. Myelin stops the charge leaking away, so the signal spike moves along faster.

FACT

Nerve signals speed to the brain at 270 km/h. End-to-end an adult human's nerves would measure 72 km.

WARNING HIGH VOLTAGE!

AN INSIGHT INTO SIGHT

Some people say the eyes are the window to the soul. They are certainly our windows onto the universe. Beams of light pushed out from atoms zing around space until they enter our eyes – and we see the world.

All light carries energy. When it enters the eye, that energy is captured by chemicals in the eye's light-sensitive back wall, known as the retina. The energized chemicals set off a process that sends nerve signals to the brain. Each nerve signal represents one dot of light. The brain puts all the dots together to make an image of what you can see.

The pupil is surrounded by the iris. Both are protected by the cornea.

Getting focused

The eyeball is a hollow ball filled with clear jelly. The light gets in through the 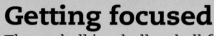 at the front. This looks like a black spot, but it is a hole into the eye (it's very dark inside). Once inside the eye, light passes through the lens. This is a flexible capsule of clear liquid. Tiny muscles stretch the lens into the right shape so the light shining through it forms a clear image on the retina. This is the same kind of process as moving a magnifying glass to get a sharp view of an object. (A blurred image can be corrected by glasses.) The optic nerve carries signals from the retina to the brain, which interprets them as sight,

SUPERHUMAN

ALHAZEN

Seeing Is Believing (965–1040)
Ancient peoples thought eyes zapped out beams of light that reflected off objects so we could see them. In Iraq, Ibn al-Haytham (also known as Alhazen) wondered how we could see distant stars easily if light had to travel from our eyes to the star and back again. He used one of the first experiments to show that light came from things like lamps, stars, and the Sun, and reflected off other objects.

FACT

Blinking keeps the cornea, the transparent cover over the pupil, clean and moist. You blink about 10,000 times a day.

The lens focuses light on the retina.

The retina at the back of the eye is made up of light-sensitive cells.

Light enters through the pupil.

Rainbow light

The three primary colours (red, blue and green) can produce all the colours of the rainbow.

The iris changes in size according to the intensity of the light.

The optic nerve connects the eye to the brain.

TRY THIS

BLIND SPOT

Test your blind spot by copying the two symbols below.

WHAT YOU'LL NEED

Two symbols
Two eyes
Sheet of paper

The retina has a blind spot where the optic nerve joins the eye. This patch cannot detect light, so it creates a hole in your vision. Usually, your brain fills the blind spots in with what the other eye sees. But this test will show you they are there. Shut your left eye, and look at the cross with your right eye. Don't look directly at the spot, just know it is there. Now edge closer to the cross. The spot will disappear: it has entered the blind spot. Try again with the left eye open, only this time look at the dot: the cross will disappear.

HEAR! EAR HERE!

Hearing is like a superpower. It works just as well in the dark, works around corners and can alert you to danger that's still miles away.

The outer ear, or pinna, collects sound waves. It focuses them into the ear canal, where they crash into a barrier of skin called the eardrum. Like a real drum, this thin layer vibrates when it is struck.

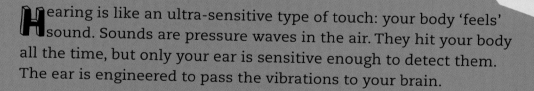

Hearing is like an ultra-sensitive type of touch: your body 'feels' sound. Sounds are pressure waves in the air. They hit your body all the time, but only your ear is sensitive enough to detect them. The ear is engineered to pass the vibrations to your brain.

Yuck!

Waxing Lyrical

The scientific name for earwax is cerumen. This sticky yellowish paste lines the ear canal to collect dust and germs before they reach the ear drum. As the wax builds up, small lumps break off and fall out of your ear. There is no real need to clean away wax: it gets rid of itself, and poking things in the ear can do more harm than good. As the saying goes, 'Never put anything smaller than your elbow in your ear.' Wise words…

Why do we have two ears? When a sound arrives at the left ear before the right, your brain can tell the source is in that direction.

RADICAL RADIO

Did you know you can hear with your jaw?

When you go swimming, your ear canal fills with water. The eardrum stops working – but you can still hear by picking up sound waves with your jawbones. You can show this works by sticking your fingers in your ears and biting a radio. Be sensible: use a battery-powered radio, not one that's plugged into the mains (only a small one will fit, anyway). Keep the volume low, and don't bite hard. The sound will get louder because you are listening with your jaw.

WHAT YOU'LL NEED

A radio
Your teeth
Common sense

WARNING
BE CAREFUL!

Boney beat

The ear includes the three smallest bones anywhere in the body: the hammer, anvil and stirrup (they're named after their shapes). They tap out the rhythm of the eardrum on the labyrinth, which is a boney chamber full of liquid. Much of the looping, twisting labyrinth is actually used to control the body's balance. The sound heads to one part of it, the snail-like cochlea. The cochlea is lined with 'hairy' nerve cells. They move in the waves pulsing through the liquid and generate nerve signals. The signals pass to the brain ... and you hear a sound. The whole process takes a tiny fraction of a second.

In the middle ear, motion from the eardrum passes through tiny bones: the hammer, anvil and stirrup. The stirrup taps a chamber filled with liquid, called the labyrinth.

The sound heads to the cochlea, which is coiled like a snail shell. Nerve cells send signals to your brain.

FACT

Your ears pop on airplanes because the air pressure in your middle ear is different from the pressure in the cabin. The pop is air being pushed in or out of the ear through a tube behind the nose.

IT'S JUST A FLAP OF SKIN AND SOME **TITCHY BITS** OF BONE!

GETTING SNIFFY

One sense organ is as plain as the nose of your face. Yep, it's your nose. While the eyes and ears detect just one thing each, the nose is a generalist. It scans the air for 10,000 different chemicals.

In the animal world, the human nose is nowhere near the top of the league. A bloodhound's sense of smell is up to 100 million times better than ours – and some bears' noses are seven times more sensitive than that.

The human ability to smell comes well done the list of super senses. We don't use it to find food like a shark does, to communicate like a dog or to detect enemies like a deer. For us, the sense of smell is really only there to warn us of rotten food or to tell us if something is burning... whether it's lunch or the house! The smell of food also fires our digestive system, making us hungry and ready to eat.

Patchy service

The sense of smell – olfaction, as the experts call it – starts in a hollow space behind the nose. Air rushing up each nostril passes over a thumbnail-sized patch of cells on the roof of the nasal cavity. The inside of the nose is covered in moist, gooey mucus (you know it as snot), which traps a sample of the chemicals fluttering around in the air. These chemicals are analyzed by 40 million receptor cells that line the cavity and are hard-wired through the skull to the olfactory bulb, the section of the brain that handles smells and works out what they mean.

FACT

The human brain devotes just 0.01 percent of its brain to the sense of smell. A shark uses 30 percent of its brain for smelling.

SNIFF
SNIFF

MMM ... SICK

Perfumes smell lovely, right? Perhaps not if you knew the ingredients. They include whale sick and cat poo. One popular ingredient is musk, which is secreted by a deer.

Hairy nose cells

The cells that pick up different scents are called olfactory receptors. They are a type of neuron, or nerve cell. The cell's dendrites (see pages 58–59) run up to its surface, where they mingle with the chemicals that have been trapped by the mucus that lines the nasal cavity. There are about 1,000 different types of receptor, each one of which detects a certain group of chemicals. When a scent chemical latches onto a dendrite, the cell fires off a signal to the brain.

BUZZ

BUZZ

Losing sense

Women and girls are better smellers than men and boys. People begin to lose their sense of smell from the age of 30 onwards; by the age of 80, they can only smell half as many odours as a young adult. Of course, a bad cold that fills the nasal cavity with gunky snot stops anyone smelling almost completely...

YUCK!

ANCIENT NOSE JOBS

The human nose has only one bone: the nasal bone, which forms a short curved ridge at the very top of the nose, between the eyes. On the outside, this bone is called the bridge of the nose. The rest of the nose is made from sheets of flexible cartilage, which is why it can squash and bend so easily. It also means it is easy to break and deform. Changing the shape of the nose is called rhinoplasty – or a 'nose job'. It was invented 3,500 years ago in India by one of the first surgeons in history, Sushruta. He rebuilt a nose that had been cut off completely using a flap of skin from the cheek.

TIP OF YOUR TONGUE

Whether you are licking a lolly or sucking a lemon, taste receptors in your mouth tell you what you are eating – and whether it might be harmful to your health.

The top tasting tool is the tongue. The upper surface of this large, super-flexible flap of muscle is covered with taste detectors. If you poke your (tongue) out in the mirror and take a close look, you might be able to spot little bumps on it. Despite what many people think, these are not the tastebuds. Each one is called a papilla. If you could look even closer, you would see that most of them are mushroom shaped. The papilla is in turn dotted with little pits. These pits are the tastebuds: you have about 5,000 of them. They detect the flavours in food.

The tongue is also a vital part of speech, helping to produce different sounds.

Under the Skin

Tastebuds

A tastebud uses several special nerve cells to detect different chemicals mixed into the saliva. Most tastebuds can pick up any of the five basic tastes. Their hair-like nerve endings poke out into the chemical-laden saliva. They detect different substances with sensors on their outer membranes.

Putting taste TO THE TEST

The tongue relies on its more powerful cousins, the nose and the eyes, for help. If you can't see or smell foods, most will taste pretty much the same. See for yourself.

WHAT YOU'LL NEED

Solid foods, like apples or potatoes

Drinks, like fizzy orange or lemonade

You need to prepare the tests first. Some solid foods to try are apple and raw potato. Cut a slice of apple and a slice of peeled potato; make them the same shape and size. For liquids, you could use fizzy orange and lemonade, poured into identical cups.

Now put on a blindfold (make sure that you can't see, and don't peek). Hold your nose firmly. Ask a friend to hand you each item at random. Try the two solid foods. Can you tell which is which? Now do the same with the drinks.

What tastes mean

The tastebuds can detect five basic tastes: sour, sweet, bitter, salty and umami (or savoury).

• Food with sugars, especially sucrose, tastes sweet. Sugar is the body's main source of fuel, so most people eat plenty of sweet things if they can.

• Salty foods contain sodium, an important mineral used in nerves and muscles.

• Sour foods have acids in them. Sourness is often a warning that food may not be good for you.

• Bitter foods come from leaves or unripe fruits. They often contain poisons that upset the stomach.

• Umami indicates the presence of useful proteins. It stimulates our appetite when we taste it.

FACT

Tasting is about 80 percent smell, and your sense of smell increases when you are hungry.

TOUCH SENSITIVE

Let's get to grips with the sense of touch. Really, this is several senses rolled into one. They are capable of feeling the shape and texture of objects, detecting forces pushing on the body and distinguishing heat and cold.

The proper name for touch is the somatosensory system. It mostly works in the skin. The dermis layer of the skin contains a range of detectors, hardwired into the nervous system. However, touch is not just skin deep; we can feel deeper inside our body with detectors in the joints and around the vital organs.

The touch detectors are often described as nerve endings. True, they are dead ends of a nerve, but they come in different shapes and sizes depending on what they are there to detect:

Sharp pains: Focused force on a small area of skin, such as a pinch, are picked up by dendrite branches of a nerve that spread into the epidermis. These fire off messages if the skin is agitated, creating a sharp pain to get your attention quickly. These pain detectors also crop up in other parts of the body.

SUPERHUMAN

LOUIS BRAILLE

Reading for the Blind (1809–1852)
Braille is a writing system that represents letters as patterns of small bumps. People who cannot see writing can read braille by touch. Each letter has between one and five dots positioned in a grid that can be 'read' with one fingertip. The system was invented by the blind Frenchman Louis Braille in 1829. Braille got the idea from 'night writing', which was used by soldiers to send messages in the dark.

TWO-POINT TEST

How sensitive are the different parts of your body? To find out, all you need is a paperclip.

WHAT YOU'LL NEED

A paperclip

Bend the paperclip into a U-shape with the ends about 2 cm apart. Now press the ends onto your skin. Can you feel two points or just one? Try this in different parts of the body, such as the palm, finger, arm, neck, calf, foot and shin. Areas with a lot of touch receptors will pick up both points, while less sensitive ones will just feel one.

Getting the vibes: Deeper detectors pick up rapid changes in the pressure of a force. These are felt as vibrations or roughness.

And stretch: At the base of the skin, more nerve endings detect if the skin is being stretched sideways. This creates a sensation of slipping, such as when sliding your finger across a table.

Feeling the heat: Thermoreceptors pick up heat and cold. Cold receptors are in the eyes, so you blink more in a cold wind. The tongue and mouth are sensitive to temperature, but the fingers have even more thermoreceptors. If something is too hot to pick up, that helps prevent you from putting it in your mouth, which is more easily damaged.

SENSORY HOMUNCULUS

The sense of touch is not evenly spread around the body. Some areas are more sensitive than others. If the body reflected the number of receptors each part has, it would look like this. Really sensitive parts, like the lips and hands, would be relatively huge.

FACT

There are 3,000 touch receptors in one fingertip.

REFLEX ACTION

Sometimes there is no time to think: everything happens by reflex action. A reflex short circuits the nervous system, cutting out the brain. Your senses and muscles work together automatically to save you from danger.

Reflexes are at work all the time, and we don't even know they are happening. That's probably just as well. Reflexes are mostly for our own protection, and without them we could get hurt a lot more often. They make us sneeze, blink and cough, they protect the ear from loud noises and stop us falling over with every step. We have some of these reflexes from birth. Others become built in like safety circuit-breakers as we learn to walk and control our bodies.

A cough clears out irritants that might damage the respiratory system.

The spinal cord is like a superhighway for nervous signals. That is why spinal injuries are often so serious.

Applying grey matter

Only a few major nerves connect directly with the brain. They are called the 'grey matter' and form the middle of the spinal cord. The rest form the outer layer of the spinal cord, known as the 'white matter' (the nerves are white, because of their fatty coats). Usually, a signal from the senses goes up the grey matter into the brain then comes back down along another nerve to a muscle. When the signal is very strong, like a sharp pain, the brain gets left out.

FACT

Brain-dead patients sometimes show the Lazarus reflex, crossing their arms across their chest even though their brains no longer function.

REFLEX HALL OF FAME

STIMULUS: Feeling embarrassed
ACTION: The face goes red. This may be linked to the fight-or-flight response. It is a signal that you feel threatened by what people might think of you.

STIMULUS: Sneeze; something irritates the lining of the nose
ACTION: Similar to a cough, but generally more powerful and through the nose. Most people's eyes shut just before they sneeze, perhaps to protect them from germs spraying out at 100 km/h.

STIMULUS: Shivering; the body temperature drops
ACTION: Large muscles twitch very quickly, to generate a bit of heat to warm you up again.

STIMULUS: Corneal reflex; something gets close to one eye
ACTION: Both eyelids blink.

KNOBBLY!

The grey matter sends the signal straight out of the spinal cord to the muscles. This short cut is known as a reflex arc. It produces movements before you know what is happening. The simplest example is a pin prick: you recoil in response before you feel much pain. All thanks to a reflex arc and a tiny bit of grey matter.

TRY THIS

TEST YOUR REFLEXES

The knee jerk helps you balance as you walk.

WHAT YOU'LL NEED
A knee
A soft hammer
A friend (whom you trust)

Sit with your feet dangling off the floor. Ask a friend to tap gently on the fleshy part of your leg just below your knee cap. The thigh muscles will contract, making your lower leg swing upward. It feels weird, but as long as you are gentle, you can do it as much as you like.

Pg 84-85

Why don't you just GROW up?

Pg 86-87

Goo Goo

Pg 78-79

Is that a YAWN or a ROAR?

Where do BABIES come from?

Pg 80-81

I don't believe in SPROUTS!

SYSTEMS

The parts of your body don't work on their own. They are joined by networks of tubes or nerves into complex systems. Each system has a particular task. Different systems protect the body from disease and control its growth; they extract energy from food and control the body in an emergency. Your body has its own ways to repair itself by sleeping – and a remarkable ability to imagine things that don't even exist.

WHO'S BEEN WRITING ON MY HEAD?

WARNING
IT ALL JOINS UP!

Pg 88-89

INVADERS ATTACK

You're under attack. Disease-causing bugs are constantly trying to get into your body. Most of the time your defences repel these invaders. If one gets through, it's time to call in the immune system.

Read more about the nose on pages 64-65.

It is not easy to get inside the human body. The best ways in are through the nose and mouth. But air-borne bugs get caught in thick nose hairs or slimy mucus. And bugs arriving through the mouth are soaked in saliva that kills them with a disinfectant.

YOUR BODY IS LIKE ARMOUR!

Organisms that make us sick are called pathogens. There are two types: viruses and bacteria. Viruses cause infectious diseases.

If we do get sick, the immune system strikes back. The system is led by white blood cells. Despite their name, these cells patrol far from the blood system through body tissues. Every cell in your body carries ID markers called antigens. White blood cells check the IDs and spot any invaders with different antigens. A white blood cell then engulfs the bug and digests it harmlessly. If you are ill, the invader – known as a pathogen – has taken over a body part. The immune system releases antibodies. These markers stick to a pathogen's antigens. That makes it easy for killer cells to track them down and finish them off.

FACT

Viruses are everywhere. A glass of seawater, for example, has more viruses in it than there are people on Earth. Nearly all are harmless to humans.

Under the Skin

Down the drain

When you are sick, lumps in your neck might swell a little. People may say 'your glands are swollen', but the lumps are actually lymph nodes. These filters, which collect pathogens for removal, are located all round the body. They are part of the lymphatic system, which runs through the body to drain liquid that leaks out of the blood. Pathogens are flushed out the same way, and killer white blood cells rush to the nodes ready for a fight, causing swelling.

LEAGUE OF INVADERS

Bacteria

Billions of these microorganism live on the skin and in the gut – and do us no harm at all. However, many germs cause illness.

Viruses

Viruses are tiny packets of protein that lodge in your cells and instruct the cell's DNA to make thousands of copies. Eventually, the cell bursts apart, releasing more viruses into the body.

Protists

Larger single-celled organisms cause diseases like dysentery (dangerous diarrhoea) and malaria, which attack the main organs.

Fungi

Yeast can infect soft tissue, causing itchiness. Other fungi cause skin diseases such as athlete's foot and ringworm.

Parasites

Many parasites can live on or inside the body.

STOP BUGGING ME!

SUPERHUMAN

EDWARD JENNER

Disease vs. Disease (1749–1823)

English doctor Edward Jenner found a way of using the body's immune system to protect it against disease. In the 1790s, he developed the first vaccine, for the deadly disease smallpox. The idea was to inject patients with a weak form of the disease that barely harmed them. The immune system tackled the injected infection easily and the patient became immune to the deadlier form of disease. All the vaccines used today work on the same principle.

HORMONE SOUP

The body's control system doesn't only rely on nerve signals to get things done. Chemical messengers called hormones also deliver commands and keep everything working just right.

Hormones are made in chemical factories called glands. Those used inside the body are manufactured in endocrine glands, which deliver them to the blood. There are about a dozen endocrine glands dotted around the body from the brain to the sex organs, and each produces specific chemicals. (Exocrine glands pump chemicals out of the body. They produce things like spit, mucus, (stomach juices) sweat and tears.)

Stomach juices are used inside the body, then pushed outside.

The main role of hormones is to keep the body working within its operational limits. In other words, they stop it from getting too hot or cold, too hungry or tired, or from running out of water. This balance is called homeostasis, which comes from the Greek meaning 'to stay the same'.

WARNING BODY AT WORK

FACT

Steroids, the drugs taken by sports cheats, copy the action of hormones. They upset the delicate balance of the body's systems – and can kill.

Under the Skin

In the loop

Hormones work by what is called a negative feedback loop. For example, when the brain senses the blood is cold, it sends more frequent commands to the thyroid to release thyroxine. This boosts the amount of hormone, lifts the metabolic rate and raises the body temperature. As the blood warms up, the brain sends fewer commands for thyroxine. The increase in hormone has created negative feedback, which results in a decrease in hormone – and eventually leads to another increase in hormone. The loop goes round and round, constantly balancing and rebalancing.

The endocrine glands produce a soup of hormones flooding in and out of the blood in response to changing conditions.

Regulating water: Antidiuretic hormone (ADH) controls the amount of water in the body. It is produced by the pituitary gland, behind the nose.

Sleeping: Melatonin is secreted by the pineal gland. It makes us feel sleepy at night and wakes us up in the morning.

Ready for action: When the body needs to get moving, adrenalin is secreted by the adrenal glands on top of the kidneys.

Fuel levels: Hormones from the pancreas control the body's glucose. If the sugar in the blood stream is too high, the pancreas secretes insulin, which makes the liver convert the sugar into glycogen to store. When blood sugar falls, the pancreas makes glucagon, which turns glycogen into glucose.

Thyroid throttle: The speed at which the body works – the metabolic rate – is controlled by the hormone thyroxine, from the thyroid gland. Among many other jobs, thyroxine is involved in controlling body temperature.

Blood Sugar TEST

How good is your body at dealing with sugar. Try eating some yummy (but not very healthy) food to find out.

WHAT YOU'LL NEED
White bread
Crisps
Fruit juice

Have a starchy lunch, such as a white-bread sandwich, crisps and a sugary drink (but not a fizzy one – remember, this is all in the name of science). Sit quietly for about half an hour. Do you feel more sleepy or more awake? All that starch has been turned into sugar in the small intestine, and the body quickly removes it from the blood. Insulin converts it to glycogen, ready to store. But insulin works too well, so the amount of sugar in the blood drops below where it should be. That will make you feel a bit sleepy and sluggish until the glucagon can restore your blood sugar to the right level… So eat a more balanced lunch next time.

SHOULD I STAY OR SHOULD I GO?

It's an emergency! What do you do? While you hesitate, your body takes over. Two adrenal glands on top of your kidneys dump a hormone named adrenalin into your blood. Within seconds your body is ready to fight ... or to run away. This is the fight-or-flight response. Its job is to keep you alive.

Adrenalin has a wide-ranging effect on the body. It shuts down nonessential processes and prepares you for anything. But don't be scared. Well, actually, do be scared. That's one of the things adrenalin is good at: it makes you scared, because being scared helps you escape from danger.

Thump, thump: Your heart beats faster and harder. The blood pump is revving the body's engine, boosting blood pressure and sending fuel and oxygen to the muscles, priming them for action.

Gasp: Your blood needs oxygen and you start to breathe more quickly to increase the supply.

ROAR!

That sinking feeling: You feel your tummy drop as muscles in your stomach and intestines relax. Their energy supply is diverted to skeletal muscles, to get you ready to move quickly.

78

Panic Stations

Experts call the fight-or-flight process hyperarousal. Whatever you call it, it's not perfect. Sometimes it hinders you rather than helps. If you breathe too fast and not deeply enough – which is called hyperventilating – not enough oxygen reaches the blood. The muscles get so pumped that they start to twitch and shake, making it hard to perform fine movements, like putting a key in a door. In the worse cases of panic, the sphincter muscles in your bladder and anus relax: that makes you pee and poo uncontrollably. Oh, and eventually you'll faint. Nice…

FACT

'Adrenalin junkies' love the thrill of being scared. They deliberately keep their bodies on edge.

Blood vessels can expand or contract to control the flow of the blood.

Feeling pumped: The blood vessels in your running and fighting muscles widen to allow more blood in. That increases the supply of sugars and oxygen, so the muscles can work harder for longer without getting tired.

Dry mouth: The salivary glands are switched off to save energy. Tasting and eating are the last things on your mind, so your mouth goes dry. The tear ducts do the same. You won't be able to cry until this is all over.

Wide eyed: The irises in your eyes open to let more light in and widen your field of vision. If anything moves, you'll see it.

Going pale: While the blood vessels in the muscles expand, those in the skin constrict. Less blood reaches the surface of the body, so you turn pale. The blood is more useful being used as fuel elsewhere.

Fuelling up: The liver starts to convert energy stores into sugar to fuel any fighting or running you need to do.

TAKING ON FUEL

Do you eat to live or live to eat? That's not a question we can answer for you, but whatever you decide you'll need to understand what is in food and what the body does with it.

People say you are what you eat. Let's see if they are right. What did you eat today? Perhaps a bowl of cereal, a banana, a sandwich and some pizza, washed down with fruit juice. Or did you eat a head, two arms, two legs ... some ears?

As you might expect, it is a bit more complicated than being what you're eating. Food is a combination of fuel that keeps you alive and raw materials that your body needs to grow and repair itself. There are three main substances you need to eat: carbohydrates (simple or complex), fats and proteins.

Some people say that there are four, if you include cellulose.

CARBS

Simple carbohydrates are called sugars. Sugar is instant energy: the body burns it. Complex carbohydrates, or starch, are found in bread and potatoes. Our bodies use the starch to make sugar – for more energy.

FATS

If more sugar comes into the system than your body needs, it converts to fat. Fats (or lipids) have various uses, but most is used an energy store. If you eat too much, you'll put on weight as fat. (The body prepares for the worst, so it stores fat in case you run out of food.)

Protein

The final food group is protein. Proteins are like toy bricks – a few pieces can be arranged into just about any shape. Proteins are made from chains of amino acids. The order of the acids defines the function of the protein, from being a muscle fibre to being an enzyme.

Cellulose

Perhaps protein is not the final food group. A complex carbohydrate called cellulose – found in green vegetables – is indigestible. But although we get no nutrition from this fibre, it helps push food through the gut ... and means we poo regularly.

VITAMINS

Vitamins are chemicals that are essential for the body but which cannot be made from other foods. There are dozens of vitamins and other minerals we need in our diet (only in tiny amounts). These are a few of the main ones: where you find them, what they do and why you cannot do without them.

FACT

Healthy women should have a little more body fat than healthy men.

Vitamin	A	B	C	D
Where?	Liver, egg yolk, carrots	Cereals, nuts	Citrus fruits, kiwi, tomatoes	Oily fish and sunshine
What foR?	Eyes, lungs, skin	Nerves, muscles and heart	Immune system, healing	Bones and teeth
What do they prevent?	Night blindness	Peri peri: brain damage and heart failure	Scurvy: bleeding gums and inelastic skin	Rickets, deformed bone

SUPERHUMAN

JUSTUS VON LIEBIG

A Fertile Idea (1803–1873)

In 1840, the German chemist von Liebig figured out the chemicals inside sugars, fats and proteins. He also found that one of the most important plant nutrients was nitrogen taken from the soil. Plants use nitrogen to make proteins, without which they cannot grow. Von Liebig suggested that nitrogen-rich chemicals could be added to soil in fertilizers to help crops grow. Today farmers use millions of tonnes of these fertilizers. Without von Liebig's idea, more than half the world's crops would not have grown.

IN AND THEN OUT

Let's take a journey ... through the digestive system. On the way we will be pulped, bathed in acid, mingled with bacteria and covered in poo.

Digestion is the process that breaks down food into small and simple ingredients that can be absorbed into the blood. The kinds of things the body is after are sugars, such as glucose, which are used as fuels; fats and oils, which are good for energy storage; and proteins, which are the building bricks of the body – and which are used just about everywhere.

Proteins are important for cell growth and repair. Read more about cells on pages 12–13.

You might think digestion is a complex and delicate process – and you'd be right. But it all starts with a bit of brute force. We begin in the mouth ... er, obviously. Food is sliced and shredded by the teeth before passing down the throat to the stomach. Already, digestive chemicals called enzymes have started to break down the food. In the stomach, the digestive chemicals are even more powerful. By now, the food is like a soup. As it passes through the small intestine, nutrients are taken out into the blood.

HALF PRICE

SPECIAL OFFER

BARGAIN

HALF PRICE

Glands under the tongue produce saliva, a watery mixture.

Strong acids in the stomach turn food into a soup of sugar, fatty acids and amino acids.

MOUTH

STOMACH

SMALL INTESTINE

Saliva makes the food slippery, so it does not damage the throat lining.

Fatty acids are found in fats. Amino acids are protein units.

A messy end

In the large intestine, things start to get really messy. Any valuable water left in the food is sucked out through the intestine wall. The solid waste that is left over is pushed out the rear opening – the anus – as a pile of poo. The bacteria in poo is what makes it unclean. If any of the bacteria find their way back into food that you eat, they may launch an attack on your intestines. They may even take over from the helpful bacteria that are already inside you. If that happens, at the very least you would get an upset tummy for a few days.

Yuck!

Passing gas

The bacteria in the large intestine make hydrogen, methane and carbon dioxide gas. The gas has to go somewhere – and it comes out as a fart. Most people fart 10 to 15 times a day. Not all farts smell. Those that do contain traces of sulphur gas, which builds up if food is not digested fully. Some foods make us more gassy than others. The chief culprits include beans, brussels sprouts and cauliflower.

ON SALE

WHAT DIGESTS WHAT?

Different enzymes work at each stage of digestion, and they break down different foods.

In the mouth: lipase digests fats; amylase digests starch; bicarbonate kills bacteria

In the stomach: pepsin digests proteins, hydrochloric acid kills bacteria, rennin digests milk

In the small intestine: bile (from the liver) digests fats; trypsin digests proteins, phospholipase digests fats, sucrase digests sucrose sugar (in fruits and sweets), lactase digests lactose sugar (in milk), maltase digests maltose sugar (in cereal)

FACT

Each of us contains about 100 trillion bacteria that help with digestion. Bacteria outnumber our own cells by about 10 to 1.

The small intestine has three sections: duodenum, jejunum and ileum.

LARGE INTESTINE

Valuable water is removed in the large intestine, leaving solid waste, or poo.

BOWEL

The small intestine breaks up food and takes useful nutrients into the blood.

A slurry of bacteria and food waste mixes with unwanted chemicals from the liver.

GROWTH: GOING UP

Here's a riddle: We've all done it. Many people wish they could get it over with. And once you stop, you'll never start again. What's the answer? Growing.

WARNING GETTING BIGGER!

Growth begins when an egg and a sperm fuse. Many years later, the (zygote) formed then becomes an adult human. Girls stop growing around the age of 17 (although the last few years are very slow) and boys stop getting any taller at about age 20. But growth is not just about getting larger.

A zygote is the single-celled organism formed when a sperm fuses with an egg.

Growth begins with a period where the body changes from a ball of cells to a set of specialized tissues and organs. Once this development has created a mini-human (a baby), the focus changes to getting bigger … and bigger. The average woman ends up about three times longer than when she was a baby (men are a little longer). And an average adult is about 20 times heavier than his or her weight as a newborn baby.

Under the Skin

Rooted in stems

Growth occurs because body cells can divide in two. But the specialized cells in the lung, kidney or retina lose the ability to divide and contribute to growth: they have other jobs to do. Instead, new cells in these areas are produced by stem cells. Any type of body cell can grow from a stem cell. Researchers believe stem cells could be used to treat all kinds of illnesses.

Powerful pituitary

The increase is size is governed by a hormone called, er, 'growth hormone'. The main thing it does is make your body longer. It turns fat stores into energy for building longer bones and muscles. To start with bones and muscles are thin as well as long: that's why children are much lankier than adults. As the process continues, growth hormone thickens the bone and makes bigger muscles. Growth hormone is made in the pituitary gland. If the pituitary gland goes wrong, people can grow very fast and for too long: this sort of rapid growth can cause health problems.

ONWARDS AND UPWARDS!

Growth scheme

Growth is fastest for the first three years of life. Another growth spurt comes at puberty, during the teenage years. This table shows the average height at different ages, and some physical characteristics.

NEWBORN BABY	50 CM	cries (often)
3 MONTHS	60 CM	smiles (sometimes)
6 MONTHS	65 CM	babbles (a lot)
9 MONTHS	70 CM	sits and crawls
12 MONTHS	75 CM	stands
18 MONTHS	80 CM	walks
2 YEARS	85 CM	runs
3 YEARS	95 CM	jumps
5 YEARS	105 CM	skips
12 YEARS	150 CM	puberty begins
17 YEARS	165 cm girls	175 cm boys

MAKING A COPY

Let's make a baby. You will need not one but two human bodies – a mother and a father. The father's sperm joins the mother's egg to make the first cell of a new person. It takes nine months or so for that cell to grow into a working human.

Goo Goo

WARNING LITTLE PERSON!

When a tiny sperm meets a giant egg cell (the largest of any human body cell), it burrows inside and adds its set of genes to the set already in the egg. That means the new cell has a different set of genes from the mother or the father. It is a zygote, the first cell of a brand new human. The mother's body changes to protect this new life. It enters a state known as pregnancy. Usually, any cell with a different genetic makeup from the body would be attacked by the immune system. However, the uterus forms a safe place for the zygote, which begins to divide into new cells very rapidly. It has only nine months to make an entire baby.

The uterus is also known as the womb. Its walls of smooth muscle protect a growing foetus.

Under the Skin

Placenta

During pregnancy a mother grows a disposable organ called the placenta. This disk transfers food and oxygen from the mother's blood to the baby through the umbilical cord. When a baby is born, the placenta follows it out. The umbilical cord is cut. The stump left on the baby dries up and falls off, leaving a wrinkled belly button or navel.

FACT
We don't know the name of Feodor Vassilyev's wife. But she gave birth to 67 children. From 1725 to 1765, she was pregnant 27 times.

FRUIT BY FRUIT

Month 1

The zygote divides into a ball of cells called a blastocyst. It floats into the uterus and implants itself into the lining of the uterus wall. It is now known as an embryo.
Size: poppy seed

Month 2

The embryo begins to form into two separate sections. One half will be the placenta. The other half is the foetus, the part of the embryo that will become the new human. By the end of the month its heart is beating.
Size: raspberry

Month 3

All the vital organs, brain and arms and legs are present in the foetus by the end of the third month. The tiny human is now connected to its mother by an umbilical cord.
Size: plum

Month 4

The foetus now has its fingers and toes, including nails. A fine coat of hair called lanugo grows on the skin.
Size: orange

Month 5

The baby begins to hear noises. It moves around in the uterus, giving kicks that show up as bulges on the mum's big tum.
Size: banana

Month 6

If the eyes aren't open yet, they will be soon. Enough light comes into the uterus through the skin for the baby to tell light from dark.
Size: lettuce

Month 7

The uterus has practice contractions. During the birth, the strong muscles in the uterus wall will push out the baby during labour.
Size: pineapple

Month 8

The baby is completely formed, but it needs to get stronger. The bones are hardening and the muscles are thickening. The last body parts are prepared for birth.
Size: coconut

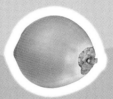

Month 9

The baby has turned head down. Its weight pushes on the cervix. Labour is triggered by a hormone from the baby. It can take many hours for the baby to pass through the birth canal (or vagina). As soon as it is out, the baby drinks from its mother's breast. It starts with colostrum. This oily yellow milk is rich in antibodies to kick-start the baby's immune system. After day or two, fatty white milk is produced.
Size: melon

JUST IMAGINE

The human body is not so different from those of other animals: A shark has a brain, too (it is V-shaped); a cricket has ears (on its knees); and a cow has a stomach (well, it has four). But the human body has something that no other animal has – an imagination.

There is a voice in your head. It is you, your mind, your self. You use it figure out problems, set goals, feel happy or sad and come up with new ideas. No one can guess exactly what another person is thinking. We use language to explain our ideas to each other, so we can work together to achieve something. In the old days, that might have been hunting a woolly mammoth. Now it might be sending a robot to Mars.

It's all in the mind

We somehow feel that the mind is separate from the body. Ancient people believed the heart did the thinking. They thought the brain was a radiator for cooling the blood. However, we now know that our thoughts, memories and emotions come from the brain. Our mind is created by many different areas of brain working together.

The brain is part of the body, but the mind is not. Read more about the brain on pages 56–57.

Under the Skin

Seeing thinking

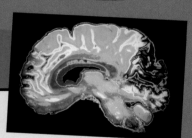

Modern medical scanners can watch a brain as it thinks. An fMRI (functional magnetic resonance image) uses magnets to follow oxygen-rich blood around the brain. When a section of the brain is active, it is supplied with oxygen and shows up on the fMRI. As well as showing which brain regions control the body, an fMRI shows how the brain thinks about different things.

We learn a lot about the way humans think from people who have injured their brains. Damaging the brain can cause problems with walking or talking. But it can also make us lose our memories, stop us from recognizing faces or even change our personalities. We make decisions using mainly the front section of the brain, which is very large compared to other animals. But how we do that depends on what we can remember from our earlier experiences – and what we learn from other people.

Power of imagination

Just as we cannot see into a human's thoughts, we don't know if other animals think like us. It is possible that only humans can imagine things that they have never seen, picture objects they will never see, or think up things that don't even exist – yet. Every now and then someone has a new idea that ends up being a new invention, a piece of art or a way of solving a problem. The imagination is perhaps the most powerful thing about the human body. Just imagine what you can do with yours!

WHO'S BEEN WRITING ON MY HEAD?

SUPERHUMAN

RENÉ DESCARTES

I Think, Therefore I Am... René Descartes (1596–1650)

Frenchman René Descartes was not well as a child. But he was very clever, so his teachers in 17th-century France let him stay in bed. Even as an adult he worked in bed. One story says that he invented graphs and coordinates while watching a fly on his bedroom ceiling. However, Descartes is just as famous for saying 'I think, therefore I am'. What did the lazybones mean? Descartes was wondering how he could tell if he really existed. But he knew that he was thinking – and that proved that he must exist. Therefore, by the way, your mind exists, too. Just think about it for a bit.

BEDTIME STORY

Humans spend about a third of their lives asleep. Sleep is necessary to give the body time to recover. You can try to stay awake, but eventually you will fall... zzzzzz₂

You are feeling sleepy. As you drift off to sleep, your breathing rate and heart slow down. Your senses are only barely working. But even while you snooze, your body still uses 90 percent of the energy it uses when it's awake. The immune system is activated to clear out invaders and any repair jobs are done faster.

While you sleep, your conscious mind is switched off and you are unaware of your surroundings. The brain is still working however. It follows a 90-minute sleep cycle. As you fall asleep, the body may twitch a little as you lose consciousness, which takes about five or 10 minutes. For the next 20 minutes you fall deeper into slumber. You then have about 45 minutes of deep sleep, where the brain function is at its lowest. If you are woken up at this stage – by a loud noise, a rough shake or a bucket of water on the head – you may feel confused for a little while as the brain gets going again.

The reason people rest when they are sick is to give the immune system more energy to repair the body.

SLEEPY TIME

Despite what you say at bedtime, children need more sleep than adults. Newborn babies sleep for 18 hours a day. Under 10s need about 11 hours, while even teenagers need more than nine hours a night.

CIRCADIAN RHYTHM

The human body works to a beat called the circadian rhythm. Each cycle lasts about 24 hours: circadian means 'about a day'. So the human body runs at the same rate as the Earth. Humans are diurnal, which means we are active in daylight and asleep at night – or at least we should be. At the end of the day, the body releases a hormone called melatonin, which makes us sleepy. When the hormone drops in the morning, we wake up. The circadian rhythm is maintained by the amount of light you see, but it takes a while to adjust. That is why if you fly to part of the world where the day and night are at different times from what you are used to, you may feel sleepy at the wrong time of day. That is called jet lag; your circadian rhythm needs to be reset.

The last 15 minutes or so of the cycle is called REM (rapid eye-movement) sleep. Until now the eyes beneath your lids have been rolling gently around. But in REM they start to quiver back and forth, and the rest of your muscles become very relaxed. REM sleep is the time for dreaming. No one knows why we dream. It may be the brain organizing new memories from the day before. It could be deep fears or desires being expressed – or it could just be random brain activity that your mind organizes into stories. Whatever it is, a dream is a normal part of the sleep cycle and nothing to worry about.

Under the Skin

Yawn!

On average we yawn 15 times day. No one really knows why. But we do know that yawning is infectious. Just reading this might make you feel like yawning. In that way, yawning is a signal to others that you need to sleep. Prehistoric people slept as a group for safety, so yawning may have been a signal for everyone to get ready for bed at the same time. A yawn sucks in a huge breath. It might be a way of removing carbon dioxide from the tired body. It might cool the brain, or the oxygen boost might wake us up a little for a very important job: finding a safe sleeping spot.

Cool Words

acid A chemical that attacks other substances, making them break apart.

alveolus One of the many tiny sacs in the lungs where oxygen is transferred from the air into the blood.

amino acid A building block of proteins; each proteins is a chain of hundreds of amino acids.

antibody A protein produced by white blood cells as part of the body's response to an antigen.

antigen A molecule on a foreign body that triggers the body's immune system.

artery A blood vessel that carries blood away from the heart.

bacteria A tiny one-celled lifeform.

bronchiole A narrow branching tube bringing air deep into the lungs.

callus A thick area of skin produced when that body part is rubbed a lot.

capillaries Tiny blood vessels that supply body cells with oxygen and fuel.

carbon dioxide A waste gas formed when the body releases energy from food.

cardiac To do with the heart.

chromosome A storage rack for a super-long coil of DNA.

collagen A flexible protein that is found in body structures such as the skin and cartilage.

conscious The condition of being awake and aware of one's surroundings.

cytoplasm The liquid inside cells.

diaphragm A sheet of muscle under the vital organs and used in breathing.

diffusion The way in which molecules of liquids and gases move from points of high concentration to points of lower concentration.

digestion The breakdown by enzymes of food into small molecules that can be easily absorbed by the stomach.

endocrine system A system of glands that releases hormones into the body.

enzyme A protein that controls a certain process in the body; enzymes can break up some substances into simple units and also join simple ones together into complex things.

fluoride A chemical in toothpaste that protects the teeth from attack by acids.

immune To be able to protect yourself from diseases.

lipid Another name for fat.

membrane A thin sheet that surrounds a cell and other structures in the body.

mineral An inorganic substance that is essential in tiny amounts for maintaining and repairing the body.

mitochondrion An organelle in every cell that releases energy from food.

neuron A nerve cell.

nucleic acid One of the building blocks of DNA; DNA contains four types of nucleic acid which create the codes we call genes.

nucleus A large bag in a cell where chromosomes are stored.

oesophagus The tube that connects the throat to stomach.

organelles A tiny structure inside a cell.

oxygen A gas in the air that the body uses to release energy from sugars and other fuels.

pathogen Something that comes into the body from outside and causes a disease; most pathogens are viruses and bacteria.

pigment A coloured chemical.

pituitary gland A gland in the brain that releases hormones that control the output of the endocrine system.

plasma The liquid part of blood.

protein A complicated chemical that is found in muscles and the skin; proteins are used as enzymes throughout the body.

puberty The time of life when a child's body develops into an adult one, capable of having children.

respiration The release of energy from food using oxygen, which takes place inside human cells. Respiration is also the term for breathing in oxygen from the air.

saliva Another name for spit.

sphincters Rounded muscles that can squeeze a body tube shut.

stem cell A special cell that can change into any type of body cell. Once it changes into a certain form, it cannot turn back into a stem cell.

urea The waste material produced from processing meat and other proteins, and which is then removed as urine, or pee.

vein A blood vessel that carries blood towards the heart.

villus A hair-like structure that sticks out from the lining of the small intestine; the villi help to absorb food chemicals more quickly.

white blood cell A colourless cell that forms an important part of the immune system.

zygote The first cell on a human body – made when a sperm and egg cell fuse together.

FIND OUT MORE

BOOKS

Amsel, Sheri. *The Everything KIDS' Human Body Book: All You Need to Know About Your Body Systems – From Head to Toe!* Adams Media Corporation, 2012.

Arnold, Nick, and De Saulles, Tony. *Blood, Bones and Body Bits* (Horrible Science). Scholastic Ltd, 2008.

Arnold, Nick, and De Saulles, Tony. *Bulging Brains* (Horrible Science). Scholastic Ltd, 2008.

Arnold, Nick, and De Saulles, Tony. *Disgusting Digestion* (Horrible Science). Scholastic Ltd, 2008.

Claybourne, Anna. *The Complete Book of the Human Body.* Usbourne Publishing Ltd, 2006.

Dungworth, Richard, Harris, Sue and Hawkins, Emily. *Pop-up Facts: Human Body.* Templar Publishing, 2007.

Green, Dan and Basher, Simon. *Human Body: A Book with Guts.* Kingfisher, 2011.

Parker, Steve. *The Human Body Book: The Ultimate Visual Guide to Anatomy, Systems and Disorders.* Dorling Kindersley, 2007.

Stowell, Louie, and Leake, Kate. *Look Inside: Your Body.* Usbourne Publishing Ltd, 2012.

Symons, Mitchell. *That's So Gross!: Human Body.* Red Fox, 2011.

Walker, Richard. *Your Amazing Body: An Interactive Journey through Your Body.* Carlton Books, 2008.

Winston, Robert. *Body: An Amazing Tour of Human Antomy.* Dorling Kindersley, 2005.

Winston, Robert. *What Makes Me?* Dorling Kindersley, 2010.

Wow! Human Body. Dorling Kindersley, 2010.

WEBSITES

kidshealth.org/kid/htbw/
The Nemours Foundation's Center for Children's Health Media Kidshealth
site page on How the Body Works, with links to many other health topics.

www.kidsbiology.com/human-biology/index.php
Children's Learning Network guide to human body systems and how they
work.

www.gosh.nhs.uk/children/general-health-advice/body-tour/
Great Ormond Street Children's Hospital kids' guide to body parts and
how they combine to form body systems.

video.nationalgeographic.co.uk/video/science/health-human-body-sci/
human-body/human-body-sci
National Geographic video entitled Human Body 101, a short introduction
to how the body works.

www.childrensuniversity.manchester.ac.uk/interactives/science/
bodyandmedicine/
A children's site run by Manchester University academics about how the
body works and how medicines can treat disease.

discovery.com/tv/human-body/human-body.html
Discovery Channel selection of three-minute videos of human anatomy in
action beneath the skin.

science.nationalgeographic.com/science/health-and-human-body/human-
body
National Geographic site named Explore the Human Body, with
simulations of body systems and how they work.

www.bbc.co.uk/science/humanbody/body/interactives/3djigsaw-02/
BBC science website page that allows you to build your own human body.

INDEX

CREDITS

Clipart: 19, 39; Getty Images: AFP 18, Hulton Archive 56; Public Domain: 42b, 65; Robert Hunt Library: 14; Science Photo Library: A Barrington Brown 30, Sheila Terry 6, Natural History Museum 69; Shutterstock: 6-7, 11, 21tr, 38bl, 42-43, 46r, 55, 84-85, 87tr, 87 cl, Africa Studio 62l, Bambook 71, Ruth Black 46l, Andrew Burgess 17, Chimpinski 63cl, Stephen Cobum 88-89, Freer 87t, Yana Gayvoronskaya 80, iprostocks 91t, Ivaylo Ivanov 87bl, Ivosar 63r, Georgios kollidas 73, Sergii Korshun 38bc, Chris Kruger 78, Ruslan Kudrin 23, Brian L. Lambert 36, Johan Larson 51b, Valery Lebedev 21, Viktar Malyshchyts 67t, Nattika 46-47b, 87blu, 87cr, Maks Narodenko 67t, Nikolay Neveshkin 37, Slavoljub Pantelic 63c, Sarunyu Foto 58-59, Bobby Scrivens 42-43c, Oleksander Semenov 46-47t, Andrey Shadrin 90br, Susan Shmitz 41, Valentyn Volkov 87br, Alexey Zet 90l, Zhukov 26; Thinkstock: Brand X Pictures 25, Hemera 88br, istockphoto 27t, 29, 62r, 89r, Photos.com 68br.
Brown Bear Books has made every attempt to contact the copyright holders. If anyone has any information please contact smortimer@windmillbooks.co.uk
All interior artworks Brown Bear Books Ltd; cover artworks Clive Goddard.

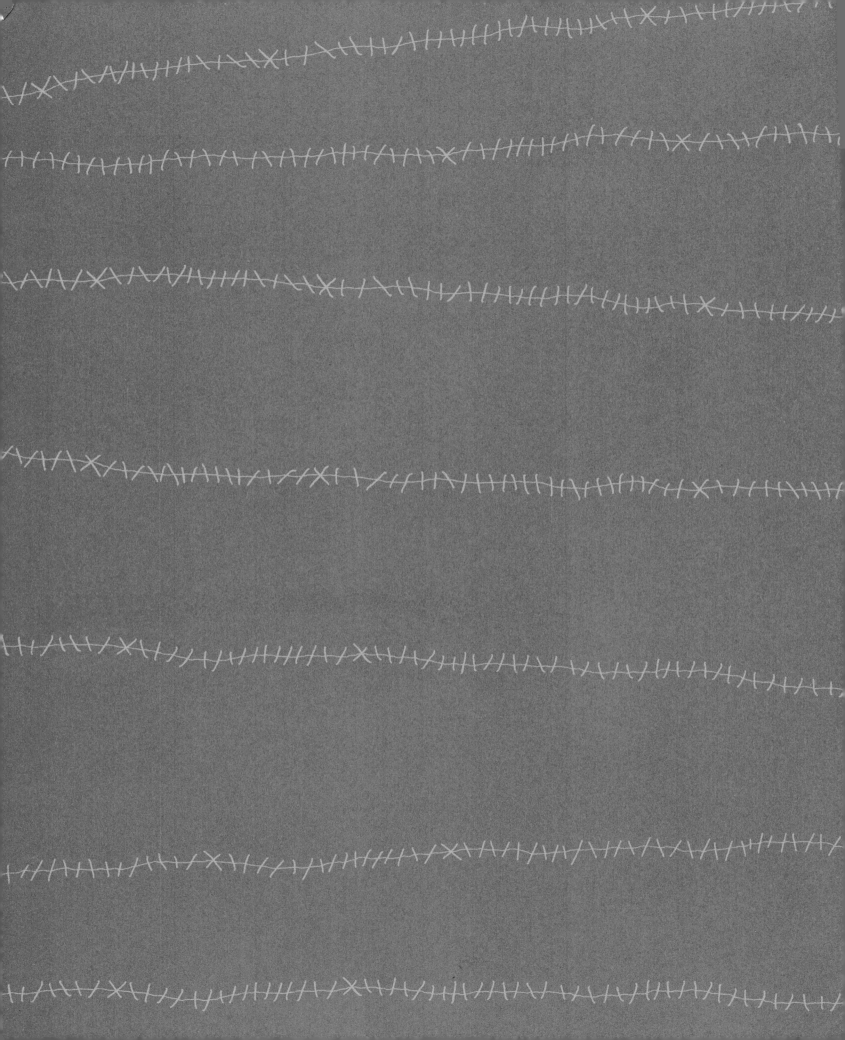